Library of Medieval Women

Agnes Blannbekin, Viennese Beguine:
Life and Revelations

Library of Medieval Women   ISSN 1369–9652

Series Editor: Jane Chance

The Library of Medieval Women aims to make available, in an English translation, significant works by, for, and about medieval women, from the age of the Church Fathers to the fifteenth century. The series encompasses many forms of writing, from poetry, visions, biography and autobiography, and letters, to sermons, treatises and encyclopedias; the subject matter is equally diverse: theology and mysticism, classical mythology, medicine and science, history, hagiography, and instructions for anchoresses. Each text is presented with an introduction setting the material in context, a guide to further reading, and an interpretive essay.

Already published

Christine de Pizan's Letter of Othea to Hector, *Jane Chance*, 1990

The Writings of Margaret of Oingt, Medieval Prioress and Mystic, *Renate Blumenfeld-Kosinski*, 1990

Saint Bride and her Book: Birgitta of Sweden's Revelations, *Julia Bolton Holloway*, 1992

The Memoirs of Helene Kottanner (1439–1440), *Maya Bijvoet Williamson*, 1998

The Writings of Teresa de Cartagena, *Dayle Seidenspinner-Núñez*, 1998

Julian of Norwich: *Revelations of Divine Love* and *The Motherhood of God*: an excerpt, *Frances Beer*, 1998

Hrotsvit of Gandersheim: A Florilegium of her Works, *Katharina M. Wilson*, 1998

Hildegard of Bingen: On Natural Philosophy and Medicine: Selections from *Cause et Cure, Margret Berger*, 1999

Women Saints' Lives in Old English Prose, *Leslie A. Donovan*, 1999

Angela of Foligno's Memorial, *Cristina Mazzoni*, 2000

The Letters of the Rožmberk Sisters, *John M. Klassen*, 2001

The Life of Saint Douceline, a Beguine of Provence, *Kathleen Garay and Madeleine Jeay*, 2001

We welcome suggestions for future titles in the series. Proposals or queries may be sent directly to the editor or publisher at the addresses given below; all submissions will receive prompt and informed consideration.

Professor Jane Chance, Department of English, MS 30, Rice University, PO Box 1892, Houston, TX 77251–1892, USA. E-mail: jchance@rice.edu

Boydell & Brewer Limited, PO Box 9, Woodbridge, Suffolk, IP12 3DF, UK. E-mail: boydell@boydell.co.uk. Website: http://www.boydell.co.uk

Agnes Blannbekin, Viennese Beguine:
Life and Revelations

**Translated from the Latin
with Introduction, Notes and Interpretive Essay**

Ulrike Wiethaus

Wake Forest University

D.S. BREWER

BV
5095
.B57
A3
2002

First published 2002
D. S. Brewer, Cambridge

ISBN 0 85991 634 0

D. S. Brewer is an imprint of Boydell & Brewer Ltd
PO Box 9, Woodbridge, Suffolk IP12 3DF, UK
and of Boydell & Brewer Inc.
PO Box 41026, Rochester, NY 14604–4126, USA
website: http://www.boydell.co.uk

A catalogue record for this book is available
from the British Library

Library of Congress Cataloging-in-Publication Data
Blannbekin, Agnes, d. 1315.
    [Vita et revelationes. English]
    Agnes Blannbekin, Viennese Beguine: Life and revelations /
translated from the Latin with introduction, notes, and interpretive
essay [by] Ulrike Wiethaus.
        p. cm. – (Library of medieval women, ISSN 1369–9652)
    Includes bibliographical references and index.
    ISBN 0–85991–634–0 (pbk. : alk. paper)
    1. Blannbekin, Agnes, d. 1315.   2. Mystics – Austria – Biography.
3. Beguines – Austria – Biography.   4. Women mystics – Austria
Biography.   I. Wiethaus, Ulrike.   II. Title.   III. Series.
BV5095.B57 A3 2002
282'.092–dc21   2001037976

This publication is printed on acid-free paper

Printed in Great Britain by
St Edmundsbury Press Ltd, Bury St Edmunds, Suffolk

Contents

For Peter Dinzelbacher

Introduction to the *Life and Revelations* of Agnes Blannbekin (d. 1315)

Biographical Background:
Agnes in the Context of the Beguine Movement

It has no doubt been more difficult for Christian women than for their male counterparts to pursue a purely religious lifestyle. Medieval European cultures defined women's proper role through their reproductive potential as mothers in a social system that privileged the rights of families over individuals and the rights of men over women. Girls were frequently married off at the onset of puberty and were expected to fit smoothly into the husband's family household economy through their domestic labor and the production of heirs to their spouses' lineage. Married women's right to own property and, once widowed, to inherit a sufficiently large proportion of wealth to keep them from a life of poverty, was severely regulated and differed widely across geographical regions and social classes.[1] Among the nobility, "surplus" daughters could be sent to a monastery with a dowry, often at a young age. Many of them used the cultural and financial resources of a monastery to develop their formidable talents as writers, composers, theologians, and educators. If a family had developed strong ties to a particular monastery, it could also use it as a safe and respectable retirement home for its widows, whose inheritance and personal wealth added to the monastic coffers.[2]

---

[1] On medieval widows, see most recently Cindy L. Carson and Angela Jane Weisl, eds., *The Construction of Widowhood and Virginity in the Middle Ages* (New York: St. Martin's Press, 1999). Widows are explicitly mentioned in chapter 139 of the *vita*.

[2] Perhaps no female writer of the Middle Ages has more eloquently described the difficulties, opportunities, and even joys of navigating through the vicissitudes of women's life stages and their options as daughters, wives, and widows than Christine de Pizan, who ended her remarkable life in a monastery that also housed one of her daughters. For an analysis of de Pizan's writings in relation to Beguine literature, see most recently Jane Chance, "Speaking *in propria persona*: Authorizing the Subject as a Political Act in Late Medieval Feminine Spirituality", in Juliette Dor, Lesley Johnson, and Jocelyn Wogan-Browne, eds., *New Trends in Feminine*

Daughters from poorer families could participate in the cloistered life as so-called lay sisters. They were not permitted to sing the daily liturgical offices in the choir like noble nuns (the so-called "choir nuns"), were only minimally educated in reading and writing skills, and had to perform the many menial tasks necessary to maintain the smooth daily operations of a monastery. Many female saints' stories tell us about a budding saint's brave refusal to get married and her determination to espouse herself to the heavenly bridegroom Christ instead. Such refusals could carry negative social consequences for the family if the daughter could not find a respectable niche, especially since for many of them admission to a monastery was not possible. Apart from a cloistered life in a well-respected monastic community, young women, widows, and sometimes even married women could try to find one or more sponsors who would support them financially if they chose to live as anchoresses. Julian of Norwich (ca. 1343–after 1416) is perhaps the best-known medieval anchoress today.[3] Her remarkable theological writings testify to the educational possibilities available to a woman who chose this path. On the other end of the anchorite spectrum, we find the sad story of Christina Mirabilis (d. 1224), who tried to pursue the life of a hermit but was brutally persecuted by villagers when she searched for a place to live outside her village. She was eventually brought back to the village, bound with iron chains, and her legs were broken. It is likely that her maltreatment was possible because she lacked sponsorship and the protection of male family members.[4]

Medieval women, whether unmarried or widowed, found a third option that gave them more independence than enclosure as a nun or anchoress could afford them: communal same-sex living with pooled resources, daily liturgical practices, prayer services for the poor, the sick, and the dead, but also relative freedom of self-governance. Eventually, members of these groups came to be named "Beguines", and their living quarters a "Beguinage". Some architectural remains of Beguinages can still be found in towns and cities today, especially in the Low Countries. Despite this common name, communities

Spirituality: The Holy Women of Liège and their Impact (Turnhout, Belg.: Brepols, 1999), 269–95.

3   See, e.g., Frances Beer, *Women and Mystical Experience in the Middle Ages* (Woodbridge, Suffolk, UK and Rochester, NY: Boydell Press, 1993).

4   See Thomas of Cantimpré, *The Life of Christina the Astonishing.* Latin text with facing English translation, translated by Margot King with assistance from David Wiljer (Toronto: Peregrina Publishing, 2nd edition 1999).

could differ in many details, from size, material well being, and rules to loose pastoral and theological affiliation with either Franciscans or Dominicans. Some women who very likely were Beguines, such as Mechthild of Magdeburg (ca. 1212–82 or 1292), also eventually joined monasteries in their old age.

The first woman recognized as Beguine by the Church is Marie d'Oignies (1177–1213), whose life has been preserved for posterity by two illustrious biographers, Jacques de Vitry (1170–1240) and Thomas of Cantimpré (ca. 1200–70). Marie's life exemplifies the spectrum of medieval Christian women's choices discussed above: she was married at the age of fourteen, remained childless, and perhaps as a consequence chose to live as an anchoress for some years.[5] Later in life she became the revered leader of a group of like-minded religious women. As is true for other Beguines, Marie's contributions as a "cultural worker" should not be underestimated. Because of her exemplary lifestyle, her experience as a married woman, and also her charisma, a woman-centered cult arose around her that sought to ensure healing and especially safe delivery during childbirth. The anonymous *History of the Church of Oignies* thus reports to us that

> In those day there flourished at Oignies that most precious pearl of Christ, Marie d'Oignies. Those who enjoyed her patronage have transmitted to posterity the story of her life, which was endowed with the virtue of many miracles. In God's name she cured the sick, cleansed lepers, and drove out demons from possessed bodies and, what is more, raised the dead. Her very clothing is in our reverent possession still. When women in labor are wrapped in it, they are freed from the danger of death and rejoice in a happy birth.[6]

We find most evidence about Beguinages in the Low Countries, northern and southern France, and Germany.[7] In Italy, a similar movement developed, although the communities rather quickly

---

[5] For a study on Beguines and women's roles as daughters and mothers, see Alexandra Barratt, "Undutiful Daughters and Metaphorical Mothers among the Beguines", in Juliette Dor et al., op. cit., 81–105.

[6] *The Anonymous History of the Church of Oignies*, translated by Hugh Feiss, in *Two Lives of Marie d'Oignies*, trans. by Margot King and Hugh Feiss (Toronto: Peregrina Publishing 1993), 265–69, quotation p. 268.

[7] The classic and still valuable study of the Beguine movement and its contexts remains Herbert Grundmann, *Religious Movements in the Middle Ages*, translated by Steven Rowan (Notre Dame: University of Notre Dame, 1995. Originally published as *Religiöse Bewegungen im Mittelalter* [Leipzig: Ebering Verlag, 1935]).

attached themselves as so-called tertiaries or Third Order to the Franciscan and Dominican orders. It is against this broadly sketched background that we can approach Agnes Blannbekin's spirituality.

The known facts of Agnes Blannbekin's life are quickly told, since our only source of information about her is her *Life and Revelations*. Her date of birth is not recorded. According to the *vita*, she was the daughter of farmers (perhaps from a village named Plambach)[8] and displayed a religious vocation early on in her life. Blannbekin learned to read but not to write, and she dedicated herself to the celibate life of a Beguine in Vienna.[9] We do not know whether she worked for a living like so many other Beguines, whether she lived alone or with other women, and whether others recognized her as a holy woman to the degree that her anonymous confessor and scribe did. Her reputation might have been ambiguous, since contemporaries sometimes derided her and thought her to be odd, for example, when she compulsively bowed toward a basement window that she passed on her way across town (chapter 44). In this incident, Agnes regained respectability only after a stolen Eucharistic wafer was discovered in the basement. On occasion, she felt wrongly accused and defamed (chapter 178).

Much of Blannbekin's autobiographical information follows well-established patterns of thirteenth-century women's mysticism: penitential exercises, fasting, eucharistic piety, visions, ecstasies, and auditions, prayers for others, and a strong attachment to the mendicant orders.[10]

The liturgical year and the reading of hours determined Agnes's daily religious activities. Personal devotional and ascetic exercises increased in frequency and intensity during the holy seasons (e.g., chapter 76). Compared to other women mystics, however, descriptions of Blannbekin's asceticism are remarkably moderate, except for the emphasis on her self-flagellation before Easter. Her daily devotional routine was organized not only temporally but also spatially.

---

[8] See Anneliese Stoklaska, "Die Revelationes der Agnes Blannbekin: Ein mystisches Unikat im Schrifttum des Wiener Mittelalters", in *Jahrbuch des Vereins für Geschichte der Stadt Wien* 43 (1987): 7–34, p. 10. Stoklaska also offers a careful analysis of the role of the scribe in the production of the text.

[9] See Peter Dinzelbacher, "Die 'Vita et Revelationes' der Wiener Begine Agnes Blannbekin (d. 1315) im Rahmen der Viten- und Offenbarungsliteratur ihrer Zeit", in *Frauenmystik im Mittelalter*, edited by Dinzelbacher and Dieter R. Bauer (Stuttgart: Schwabenverlag, 1985), 152–78.

[10] Walter Simons, "The Beguine Movement in the Southern Low Countries: A Reassessment", *Bulletin de l'institut historique belge de Roi* 59 (1989): 63–105.

She seems to have known the schedule of Masses in all Viennese churches, and is depicted as visiting church after church to attend as many Masses as possible. After Mass, she engaged in a devotional act especially dear to her but somewhat risqué, given that women were forbidden to transgress the spatial boundary surrounding the altar. Agnes had the bold habit of approaching the altar after Mass to kiss it with a great display of emotion, frequently followed by paranormal sensations (see, for example, chapter 40). Her usurpation of masculinized space is repeated and symbolically enhanced in a provocative vision, where she sees her own faith as a beautiful young woman dancing around an altar (chapter 211).

We also learn from her scribe that like him, she suffered from spells of sadness (e.g. chapters 79–84, 185), that she endured frequently intense pain (e.g. chapters 106, 208, 209), and that she enjoyed theological reflection (e.g. chapter 108). She proved to be a trusted advisor to her confessor (chapter 171) and taught him about spiritual matters (chapter 180). She was a source of comfort not only to him but also to others in their circle (see, for example, chapters 227–28). Friends and companions of both sexes are mentioned with such frequency that we gain the picture of a lively religious subculture comprising Franciscans, encloistered nuns (chapter 137) and religious lay women, some of whom were Beguines (see chapters 41, 139, 142, 143, 144). Not everybody in this group was of an urban "bourgeois" background. At least one of the Franciscans, like Agnes, was of peasant stock (Friar Otto, chapter 39), and the confessor acted at times on behalf of the duchess who appears to have been part of the circle, perhaps as benefactress (chapters 142–43).

Given the many complaints about the human imperfections of the Viennese religious community in the text, whether among its male or female members, we can almost palpably feel the struggle to create and maintain passable standards of religious conduct. Among the woes that affected the community we find a priest who raped a young woman and then celebrated Mass in a state of impurity (chapter 41). Lecherous confessors were titillated by unnecessary inquiries about the sexual practices of their confessants (chapter 71). A promising young monk escaped the Franciscan house in the middle of the night, taking some money with him (chapter 107). The bishop imposed an unjust interdict (chapter 169); and at least according to the book, there was too much jesting and joking among the friars (e.g. chapter 117). Last, but not least, a Beguine was criticized for succumbing to the material pleasures of the court (chapters 142–43).

As the *vita* tells us, Agnes Blannbekin died in Vienna on May 10,

1315. All traces of her anonymous confessor are lost, but we know the name of someone who copied his manuscript perhaps as early as 1318, a scribe by the name of Ermenrich.

Scholarly Interpretations

Although the text of Agnes's *Life and Revelations* paints such a lively picture of daily life in a religious subculture, modern scholars and writers have ignored the richness of Blannbekin's accounts in favor of a select few of her visions that challenged their own norms and world-view. The following quotations may serve as illustrations of such selective appropriations of the *Life and Revelations*: "Agnes Blannbekin, a Viennese Beguine, d. 1315, provides repulsive proof of the impact of the imagination on female visionaries"; her visions are "more than questionable", "unusual and exotic [*befremdlich*] in their bizarre character", of "strongly obscene mystical content". The mystic herself is "scurrilous" and "adventurous", a "vacuous [*blutleer*]" yet "delicious" Viennese virgin.[11] These unfavorable interpretations have only recently been replaced by a younger generation of medievalists, whose views no doubt have been shaped by greater appreciation for the cultural achievements of medieval Christian women mystics and the impact of the feminist "third wave".

In stark contrast to earlier approaches, recent studies have praised her visions for their "poetically amazing descriptive images". She herself is lauded as an "accomplished writer", "advanced" in her use of mystical metaphor; rather than being an eccentric, she is now defined as "solidly loyal in faith and practice to the institutional church".[12]

The fault lines of the current interpretive approach to Blannbekin's accounts lie not in the area of female religious respectability, but in contemporary Western concerns about female power and authorial independence. Concomitantly, we find a focus on issues of social dissent and the related question of mysticism as an

---

[11] Quoted in Peter Dinzelbacher and Renate Vogeler, *Leben und Offenbarungen der Wiener Begine Agnes Blannbekin (d. 1315)* (Göppingen: Kümmerle Verlag, 1994), 36–39.

[12] "Poetically amazing . . . accomplished . . . advanced": Albrecht Classen, "The Literary Treatment of the Ineffable: Mechthild of Magdeburg, Margaret Ebner, Agnes Blannbekin", *Studies in Spirituality* 8 (1998): 162–87, quotation pp. 181 ff. "Solidly loyal . . .": Bernard McGinn, *The Flowering of Mysticism: Men and Women in the New Mysticism (1200–1350)* (New York: Crossroad, 1998), 180.

expression of medieval (female) emancipation. Thus, scholarly evaluations of the 1990s tried to gauge the degree of influence of
Blannbekin's anonymous confessor, who put into writing and also
commented upon her orally communicated experiences, stories and
insights (see, e.g., chapter 92). As can be expected, opinions range
from the claim of Blannbekin as sole author to speculations about the
authorial dominance of her confessor/scribe to the point of his
erasure of any specifically "feminine" perspective from Agnes.[13] A
related concern is that Blannbekin was not accustomed to Latin,
which removed her even further from the scribe's sphere of influence. In this case, however, it might be of some comfort that the
scribe's Latin, in Dinzelbacher's words, is "not only simplistic, but
. . . simply bad".[14] I like to think that it is of such inelegant quality
exactly because its grammatical and rhetorical structure is so close to
Middle High German and thus Blannbekin's and her confessor's
language of conversation and exchange. It might be another clue that
much of the text was written during or immediately after a meeting
between the two, especially given the fact that much of its
compositional structure is in the form of a "diary".[15] It seems that the
events recorded are listed without a uniform overarching
compositional intent. Apart from the first few chapters which are
programmatic in character, they generally follow the flow of the
liturgical year and reflect the random patterns of town scandals,
unrest caused by military conflicts, times of illness and health,
emotional ups and downs, and so on. I know of no other medieval
text that reflects the format of a diary in quite this way.

The quest for authorial independence in medieval women's literature, however, can miss two significant issues. The first is that in our
need to counteract centuries of misogyny, we may become blinded to
the fact that despite their inferior social position, medieval women,
like their male counterparts, were still moral agents. Medieval
women, like medieval men, had the choice to support or subvert
Christianity's efforts to marginalize and persecute groups such as

---

[13] Classen (op. cit.) unambiguously assumes Blannbekin's sole authorship;
Anneliese Stoklaska (in "Die Revelationes der Agnes Blannbekin", pp. 16 ff.)
bemoans the textual erasure of any "feminine" perspective.

[14] Dinzelbacher and Vogeler, *Leben und Offenbarungen der Wiener Begine Agnes
Blannbekin*, 16.

[15] McGinn claims that the text was composed after her death, but there is nothing in
the ms. to support his view. He probably mistook the final statement by Ermenrich
to reflect on the text as a whole. See McGinn, op. cit., 18.

homosexuals, lepers, Jews, and people of color. Thus we find Agnes repeating the widely known legend about the death of sodomites at the birth of Christ (chapter 193–94). She repeatedly condemns Jews (chapters 181, 190, 193–94), presents a negative portrayal of Ethiopians and associates dark skin with evil (chapters 205, 122, 123), and interprets leprosy as a sign of moral corruption (chapter 28). When read from the perspective of any of these marginalized groups, Agnes's religious beliefs are put into sharp relief as an example of Christian hegemonic strategies, often successful, to employ its subaltern members to its own ends.

The second issue overlooked easily is the importance of literary genres in the construction of authorial personae. Blannbekin's *Vita et revelationes* is exemplary of a distinctly medieval genre in the history of Christian women writers: the co-authored devotional text. Illiterate, semi-Latinate or non-Latinate female religious specialists would dictate revelations, autobiographical reflections, letters, and devotional teachings to male and sometimes female scribes, who often, but not always, also served as the female specialist's confessor, secretary, mentor, or pupil. It is still a matter of contention to what degree of precision the textual influence of male scribes can be categorized and classified. No doubt, each case of such collaboration must be studied carefully to determine the extent to which a female mystic and visionary controlled the final written product.[16]

As the product of a collaborative process, such devotional texts take a complex transitional position between oral transmissions of religious knowledge and the single-authored literary texts to which we are used today. For reason of their unique mode of production, co-authored texts demand special attention, yet they also deserve to be treated as legitimate literary outlets for medieval Christian women. Other female authors besides Blannbekin who employed male scribes include the German visionary Hildegard of Bingen (1098–1179), the Italian holy women Angela of Foligno (1248–1309) and Catherine of Siena (1347–80), and the English lay woman Margery Kempe (ca.

---

[16] Joan M. Ferrante analyzes other forms of literary cooperation between men and women, especially cases in which women functioned as patrons of a male writer or instigated a particular writing project on a topic of their interest. The frequency of these female/male collaborations on literary texts should challenge the relevance of traditional notions of singular authorship in the analysis of these texts; see Joan M. Ferrante, *To the Glory of her Sex: Women's Roles in the Composition of Medieval Texts* (Bloomington and Indianapolis: Indiana University Press, 1997). See especially pp. 39–68 for a religious context.

1373–1438), to name just a few.[17] Clearly, the practice of co-authorship transcends not only boundaries of gender, but also of religious orders (it can be found among the Benedictines, the Dominicans, the Franciscans), of class (noble, peasant, bourgeois), of geography, and of the divide between laity, monks, and clerics.

The *Life and Revelations* of Agnes Blannbekin exemplifies several characteristics of this widely used hybrid genre. These include the admiration a male scribe often voiced for his female co-author. Unusual also is the close cooperation between two celibate members of a Church which judged any encounter between men and women as potentially dangerous and sinful and the authority each role permitted.[18] Also worthy of attention are the points of contact between stereotypically "learned" (celibate, male, clerical) and "experiential" (female, monastic, Beguine, or lay) approaches to medieval spirituality and theology, and, finally, the complex ways in which women's voices survived in and became part of the written heritage of medieval Christian culture.

In Agnes's case, her anonymous scribe identified himself only as a "most insignificant and unworthy Brother of the Franciscan Order" (preface).[19] He disclosed himself as her confessor (chapter 38). According to his testimony, Agnes repeatedly resisted sharing her extraordinary mystical experiences with him, and only after requesting and receiving affirmative signs from the Divine did she proceed to pass information on to him. "And although she was strengthened by God through such signs, she almost always talked to me with fear and shyness, prompted by me with frequent requests" (chapter 38; see also chapter 37).[20]

The Franciscan scribe's image of an ever-reluctant Agnes reproduces the humility formula required of female visionaries and should

---

[17] On Angela of Foligno, see Catherine M. Mooney, "The Authorial Role of Brother A. in the Composition of Angela of Foligno's Revelations", in *Creative Women in Medieval and Early Modern Italy: A Religious and Artistic Renaissance*, edited by E. Matter and John Coakley (Philadelphia: University of Pennsylvania Press, 1994), pp. 34–64.

[18] McGinn judges this to be "one of the most remarkable characteristics of the new mysticism of the later Middle Ages", op. cit., p. 18.

[19] On the Franciscans in late thirteenth-century Vienna, see Peter Dinzelbacher, "Die Wiener Minoriten im ausgehenden 13. Jahrhundert nach dem Urteil der zeitgenössischen Begine Agnes Blannbekin", in *Bettelorden und Stadt. Bettelorden und städtisches Leben im Mittelalter und in der Neuzeit*, edited by Dieter Berg (Werl: Dietrich Coelde Verlag, 1992), 181–91.

[20] *Et quamvis tot indiciis confortata a domino, tamen quasi semper cum timore et verecundia mihi referebat et exacta a me precibus frequenter.*

not necessarily be taken at face value. It protected both Agnes and her confessor from possible slander about their frequent contacts. It would be more surprising if the formula was missing, because in that case, both Agnes and her confessor would have violated medieval communal standards of appropriate public self-representation. The almost exclusive focus on Blannbekin, the fact that conversations are reported verbatim, and the many instances in which Blannbekin is depicted as an outspoken religious agent and observer suggest strongly that the relationship between scribe and visionary was mutually desired. Frequently, chapters include matters of subjective "feminine" concern, such as Blannbekin's own psycho-spiritual pregnancy (chapter 195), her hesitation to leave her house at night and go into the street (chapter 127), and her fear of getting crushed by the Maundy Thursday crowds because of her lack of physical stamina (chapter 75). On a material level, medieval confessors were financially reimbursed for their services; the mendicants especially received gifts and alms from the women in their care. These financial and material transactions contributed to greater equity in their relationships with female visionaries, authorial and otherwise (see chapters 166 and 167 for a description of Agnes asking friars to read Mass for her and to share bread and wine with her).

Agnes determined the textual content more than the humility formula would let us believe, yet the process of textual production no doubt also left leeway for the scribe's own concerns. Whatever the medieval scribe's influence on the *Life and Revelations* might have been, however, it pales in comparison not only to a modern devaluation of Blannbekin's spirituality, but also to the unusual act of eighteenth-century censorship in response to the first printed edition of the *Life and Revelations* in 1731. Immediately after its publication, efforts began to (and eventually succeeded in) withdrawing the text from the public and putting it under lock and key. No doubt, Blannbekin's critical comments about the papacy and immoral priests and monks contributed to the confiscation of the first edition of her works, despite the fact that the book appears to have found immediate appeal among Catholic and Protestant readers alike. A pamphlet printed in 1735 noted the visions' "superstitious" and "unusual" content, which jarred baroque Catholic sensibilities.[21] Perhaps the censors were also irked by Blannbekin's usurpation of masculinized space, such as in her practice of kissing the altar, in her

---

[21] See Dinzelbacher, *Leben und Offenbarungen der Wiener Begine Agnes Blannbekin*, p. 35.

frequent peregrinations around and about town, and in her daring to direct her gaze upon countless nude men of the cloth, one of them even dancing with naked girls in heaven (see chapters 227 and 228).

In remarkable contrast, yet also distinct from the medieval text itself, which does not make this claim, recent American scholarly opinion approvingly subsumes Blannbekin's views under the broad category of "Beguine mysticism". To quote: "basically, this Viennese Beguine [Agnes] is a good illustration of how the major themes of Beguine life and spirituality, pioneered at the beginning of the thirteenth century were alive and well – even well-respected – in the early fourteenth century".[22] Although more sympathetic than earlier evaluations, this generalization nonetheless reflects a problematic interpretive stance, since the Beguine movement is not yet fully understood in all of its social, geographical, and historical variations.

Apart from questions of social and regional distinctions, it still needs to be determined how far the specific characteristics of the new orders and their care for Beguine communities affected individual Beguines' spirituality. Mechthild of Magdeburg, who is usually identified as a Beguine, nurtured close ties to the Dominican order and later on to the Cistercians; Marguerite Porete was also close to the Dominican order, but nothing of the sort can be asserted for the Beguine Hadewijch. Although Blannbekin identified closely with the Franciscans in Vienna, she displayed very few of the "typically" Franciscan spiritual tenets, nor is there much mention of the bridal mysticism usually associated with the three best-known Beguine writers. Especially noteworthy is her seemingly un-Franciscan lack of emphasis on poverty and compassion for the poor.[23]

Austrian scholars are more hesitant than their American colleagues to see the Beguine Blannbekin as exemplary of a women's movement that has left hardly any historical evidence in Austria apart from her text. The only other Austrian mystic known to us today is a recluse by the name of Wilbirg of St. Florian, a contemporary of Agnes Blannbekin; an anonymous Viennese Beguine is

---

22 See McGinn, op. cit., p. 180.

23 Female Franciscan tertiaries, however, did not take a vow of poverty like the Friars Minor, and so it should come as no big surprise that this issue is rarely mentioned in Blannbekin's spiritual teachings. See Roberta Agnes McKelvie, *Retrieving a Living Tradition: Angelina of Montegiove, Franciscan, Tertiary, Beguine* (St. Bonaventure: The Franciscan Institute, 1997), pp. 19 ff. McKelvie's study of Angelina's life underscores the difficulties in isolating specific "Beguine" characteristics for the Italian region (chapter 3).

mentioned in a document of 1314.[24] To summarize, as the brief survey of various scholarly viewpoints demonstrates, the text of Blannbekin's mystical experiences and teachings in the end exceeds any interpretive stance that attempts to subsume its richness under just one guiding category.

When the book appeared in print in 1731, her vision of Christ's foreskin challenged not only sexual prudishness but Church teachings that it had remained on earth and that pieces of it could be seen and were venerated in several churches across Europe. The printed edition disappeared due to ecclesiastical censorship, and it is only because of the very recent efforts of two contemporary Austrian scholars, Peter Dinzelbacher and Renate Vogeler, that a critical edition of Agnes's life and revelations has become available again to a broad audience.[25]

Manuscript Sources of the Critical Edition

Blannbekin's visions survive in three types of sources. First, in medieval manuscript fragments found in contemporary collections of excerpts from various medieval mystical texts; second, in a now lost Middle High German fragment which might have been a translation from the Latin; and thirdly, in the *editio princeps* for Dinzelbacher and Vogeler's edition, the censored Latin printed edition of a carefully transcribed eighteenth-century Latin copy made by the Benedictine scholar Bernhard Pez (1683–1735) and his assistants in Melk. My translation is based on Dinzelbacher and Vogeler's critical edition of the eighteenth-century printed version, which they edited with careful attention to Pez's transcription as well as to the surviving medieval manuscripts. In general, the chapter titles appear to stem from the original medieval sources. The punctuation follows

---

[24] See Anneliese Stoklaska, "Weibliche Religiösität im mittelalterlichen Wien unter besonderer Berücksichtigung der Agnes Blannbekin", in *Religiöse Frauenbewegung und mystische Frömmigkeit im Mittelalter*, edited by Peter Dinzelbacher and Dieter R. Bauer (Köln and Wien: Böhlau, 1988), pp. 165–84. On medieval women in Austria, see Herwig Ebner, "Die soziale Stellung der Frau im spätmittelalterlichen Österreich", and Wilhelm Brauneder, "Frau und Vermögen im spätmittelalterlichen Österreich", in *Frau und spätmittelalterlicher Alltag*, edited by M. Heinrich Appelt (Wien: Verlag der Österreichischen Akademie der Wissenschaften, 1986), pp. 509–53, 573–87.

[25] Dinzelbacher and Vogeler, *Leben und Offenbarungen der Wiener Begine Agnes Blannbekin*. For further information on the primary sources, see Dinzelbacher's thorough discussion on pp. 17–38. My summary is based on his work.

modern grammar. Because of space limitations, I have left out less than a dozen chapters that repeat themes already addressed in other chapters; all except one of those chapters exclude Agnes's presence in the text and focus instead on the life and conduct of priests and friars. In order to preserve some of the flavor of the original Latin, I have chosen to stay as close as possible to the medieval text, which has inevitably resulted in some awkward and less-than-elegant phrasings. My translation is intended only as a guide to the medieval source, since no translation can capture all the nuances contained in the original. It is my hope that it will spark interest in Austrian medieval spirituality and generate more work and reflection on the life and work of Agnes Blannbekin and her unknown confessor.

The *Life and Revelations* of the
Viennese Beguine Agnes Blannbekin
(d. 1315)

Preface of the Author of the *Life and Revelations* of the Venerable Agnes Blannbekin

I praise you, Father, Lord of Heaven and Earth, that you have hidden these things from the wise and clever and revealed them to the little ones, since this [choice] was pleasing to you.

Truly, Lord, your testimonies have gained abundant credibility since you engage in conversation with ordinary people and since you have said, "I shall lead them into solitude and I shall speak to their heart." Also, it pleases you to reveal secrets to your little and humble ones. As you have done in the days of old for the forefathers in the Books of the Prophets, you disclose the unknown and hidden [aspects] of your wisdom in order to edify and console believers. You speak in manifold ways about the secrets of your mysteries with ordinary people, whom you have led into the solitude of interior contemplation.

Therefore, Blessed Trinity, I, a most insignificant and unworthy Brother of the Franciscan Order, give thanks to your venerable majesty, worthy of devotion and love, and to your truth and goodness. I will record for your praise, glory, and honor and for the edification of faith, the nurturing of devotion, and the stimulation of love for God which I have learned or will learn from the holy and trustworthy persons to whom you, Lord, have revealed yourself.

I implore you, Father of Light, whose every gift is excellent and whose every present is perfect, that you will give me the helpful wisdom of your Kingdom so that it may be with me, work with me, write with me so that I will write what is acceptable to you and so that I will not exceed the limits of truth. Amen.

Chapter 1. Concerning the Elements, Created Beings, and Objects

Since the hand of God came upon a holy person after Mass in church, she began to lose her strength with a sensation of sweetness. Experiencing raptures and enfolded in unspeakable light, she saw a man, handsome before the sons of man, and in that man she saw that light. And in the man and the divine light, she saw the elements, and creatures and the things made thereof, the small and the big, distinct in such great luminosity that it seemed that each, no matter how small, shone a hundred times brighter than the sun. As the sun shines, so does even the smallest grain or stone. And the clarity of the sun as it is now would be judged dark in comparison, much like the moon when it is hidden by a cloud. The created things were so distinct in their brightness that each was different according to its characteristics, so the green seed, and the red rose, and so the others.

Among all elements and created objects, the earth was especially bright, the reason being that God assumed His body from the earth, and that the bodies of the saints are taken from the earth, and that during the Lord's passion, the earth was soaked in the blood of the Savior and the saints. All of this was [revealed] in that man, that is, Christ.

Chapter 2. Regarding the Human Beings who will be Saved

In that place, she also saw all the human beings who still live on earth, and as she understood, she saw there was nobody but those who were to be saved, and she recognized all, even those whom she had never [before] seen. She also observed the conversion and ascension of those people to God, and how they turned first toward God. And she told me the manner of my conversion, [just] as it was.

Chapter 3. Regarding the Progress of all People

She also saw all human beings' progress in grace, which she called the ascent in God. And this ascent was miraculously erected upwards through a measure of steps. Yet she also saw that next to the ascent of the virtues, the record of the sinful states could be found, in which they once existed. In this (ascent), God's goodness manifested itself. She saw that of those who ascended, some would fall into sin. She saw the cause of the fall, and was shown the fact and the manner in which they would recover.[1] And although all were in Christ and in God, she saw some, however, closer to and more intimate with God than others.

Chapter 4. Regarding the Dwellings and Glory of the Chosen in the Fatherland[2]

In the aforementioned vision and light, she saw the dwellings and the glory of the chosen in the fatherland, that is, how all exist and are

---

1   *Resurrecturos.*
2   Blannbekin and her confessor scribe consistently use *patria* as a term for heaven or paradise to mark the existential sense of exile and alienation, even though much affirmation of the goodness of creation can be found throughout the text, most programmatically so in chapter 1. See also chapter 63. For a scriptural reference, see, e.g., Philippians 3:20.

maintained in God; and although all existed in God, some were closer to God according to the intensity of their love.

Chapter 5. Regarding the Wounds of Christ as a Whole

She saw the blessed wounds of Christ inexpressibly glorified, translucent and radiating in a clear light so that in their presence, all the chosen were permeated by the light and made translucent. Regarding the wounds of the head, she said that there were many punctures. From one single puncture, an inexpressible light flowed toward the saints so that the chosen were willing to forgo all the joys of the fatherland except for the vision of God rather than to be without the sight of Christ's blessed wounds.

She said about this light that the light of the wounds surpassed the light of the sun a thousand times, that is to say immeasurably. She said that in the sight of this light all that is desired, all that is searched for will be found and possessed.

Chapter 6. Regarding each of the Five Wounds of Christ in Particular[3]

She said that the wound of the right hand signifies the gifts which Christ dispenses to the saints here and in the fatherland. The wound of the left hand holds the saints. Spiritual refreshment flows from the wound at His side, the sweetest and most desired by all saints in the fatherland and among those who are on the way. And some drink from the stream of such delight[4] very closely, even with the mouth pressed to the side. She said that some travelers[5] drink the salutary nectar. They are closer to Christ's side than some in the fatherland.

The wound of the right foot signifies levity, not heaviness or agility. The wound of the left foot signifies the possession of joy and happiness, what we call the "three-step" − not that there is a

---

3　This mode of classification, as with the text's innumerable scriptural references, suggests that the confessor scribe was exposed to solid scholastic training, and that Blannbekin as well was steeped in knowledge of scripture, theology, and the liturgy − yet to what degree each person's expertise contributed to the overall text is impossible to determine.

4　*Voluptas.*

5　I.e. those still living on earth. It is possible that this term also refers to St. Bonaventure's model of spiritual progress as a journey to God, although Blannbekin's spirituality is organized along other parameters than Bonaventure's *itinerarium mentis in Deum.*

"three-step" or dance in the way that this word denotes a festive event among us, but she could not offer another similarity.[6]

Chapter 7. Regarding the Catholic Faith in the Fatherland

She said that in the fatherland, the catholic faith consists of light and that it shines for the saints, that is the more someone now possesses the light of faith, the more Divine light the person will have in the fatherland. Love is the price.

Chapter 8. Regarding those who are Glorified in the Body[7]

In the fatherland, she saw many who already possessed a glorified body: [those] from the New Testament, the Blessed Virgin, Mother of the Lord, and her bridal escort, Blessed John the Evangelist. She saw fully glorified the bodies and souls of the saints of the Old Testament who were resurrected with the Lord in His resurrection. And they are already glorified in body and soul, and especially those famous saints of the Old Law such as Moses and Jeremiah and others.

Chapter 9. Regarding the Superior Merits of the Blessed Virgin

The Blessed Virgin enjoys three superior qualities above all the elect. The first is that she loved and still loves God more fervently than any of the saints [love Him]. And for this reason, she has been received in God before all and above all. And the elect participate in the abundance of her love and receive the beginning of her salvation and conversion, as well as those who are still on the way. The second is that she herself is a mirror of the divine Christ and that He Himself mirrors Himself as in a mirror, conscious that He received His flesh from her. And though all saints receive their joy from the divine Christ in their fatherland, He Himself on the other hand experiences special joy through His virginal mother, since, as has been said, He mirrors Himself in her. The third is that the Blessed Virgin was

---

6   Associating Christ with dance is an ancient Christian tradition. See Hugo Rahner, *Man at Play* (New York: Herder & Herder, 1972), chapter 4, and again Blannbekin, chapters 211, 222, 227, 228.

7   Medieval European Christianity was fascinated with the notion of a glorified body; medieval theology and mysticism developed several models that imagined the looks, functions, and meaning of such a body, which was far superior to its terrestrial prototype. See Caroline Bynum, *The Resurrection of the Body in Western Christianity* (New York: Columbia University Press, 1995).

installed as a mediator between God and sinners in order to pacify and to reconcile God. And everyday, for this reason, her renown increases through those who through her merit and intercession are converted and make progress in becoming good persons.

Chapter 10. Regarding the Crowned Saints and after that, Regarding Confessors

She saw the saints crowned according to their reward, outwardly[8] and in several ways. That is to say the confessors wore crowns that surrounded them from the feet up and around so that they seemed crowned from every angle. And yet the same crown crowned their head, and it was divided into four parts so that it seemed golden in the front, red in the back, green on the right, and on the left the color of the sky. These colors signified the confessors' merits.

Chapter 11. Regarding the Crown of the Martyrs

The crown of the martyrs was [colored] red through and through and suspended high above their heads without touching the head, much like the crown of the confessors, although it enveloped them everywhere without touching them.

Chapter 12. Regarding the Crown of Virgins

The crown of virgins was distinguished by many colors and was incredibly beautiful as it was adorned with four types of flower, roses and lilies, violets and flowers of the field. And this crown was closer to the head, yet without touching it, as was not the case with the other crowns. She said that those crowns were formed by God's gaze and

---

8 Blannbekin's emphasis on classifying visual data and human behavior according to external and internal dimensions reflects a medieval sensibility towards the phenomenal world as charged with multiple levels of meaning, some of them esoteric, that resist immediate, "literal" decoding. Related to this is also her attention to portentous weather patterns and animal behavior (see especially chapter 122), and the supernatural beings' use of costume to make a point. This mode of cognition and perception has received sophisticated metaphysical elaboration by medieval mystical theologians in the Christian tradition, including Franciscans such as St. Bonaventure. However, Christians also used it with great polemical force against Jews, who were defamed as incapable or unwilling to move beyond a literal dimension of decoding the natural world and, by extension, sacred scripture. See chapter 23 for an ecstatic experience that moved Agnes beyond the material level of spiritual delight.

their looking back at each other, that is, how they saw themselves being looked at by God.[9] And from that Divine gaze, the merits of each of them were legible in their crowns as if they were written down with letters. Those crowns signified the merits of external devotional practices. Therefore, those who were more experienced [i.e. of higher rank] had outwardly more decorations and beauty on their crowns. Yet the interior merits, as she said, were [evaluated] according to the strength of charity. The rewards of these interior merits were greater amicability and familiarity with God.

Therefore, as she said, some martyrs surpass each other according to their merits and rewards. She said that some who had suffered more extensively and arduously than others had the more shimmering crowns, even more so than those who had greater familiarity with God. And other martyrs, who suffered less than others, yet with more charity, were closer and more familiar with God, but outwardly had crowns that were not as shiny as the crowns of martyrs who had suffered more, yet with less charity.

Chapter 13. Regarding the Blessed Virgin's Crown of Twelve Stars

Regarding the glory of the Blessed Virgin, she said that she was dressed with the sun and had a crown of twelve stars on her head and the moon under her feet. She explained this as follows: she said that they were not stars like [those] in the firmament, but that any other name or similitude could not describe them. And there in the fatherland, they are declared to be stars, and there they were distinguished from each other according to their clarity and significance. Each one of them represented certain honors, merits, and virtues of the Blessed Virgin, which can be understood by the rational mind through the very look of these stars.

The first symbolizes that she is the daughter of the eternal Father and that through her, the Father is honored by a multitude of believers who through her are made adoptive sons of God. The second expressed that she is the very mother of the sons of the eternal God and His own according to her interior love. The third star expressed

---

9   Medieval European theories of vision, similar to other world cultures, assumed that a physical, energetic reality would be tapped into and created by the gaze and the act of perceiving images. This chapter is a very explicit example of the positive reality-creating nature of a gaze; the concept of an "evil eye", i.e. the harm done by evil looks, is its better-known ethical counterpart. See Gudrun Schleusener-Eichholz, *Das Auge im Mittelalter* (München: W. Fink, 1985).

that she is the bride of the Holy Spirit in the great, no, greatest union with God before all other saints. The fourth star expressed that she is the queen of angels and [represents] the greatest love that the holy angels have for human beings and that thanks to her, the fall of the angels is restored through humankind. The fifth star expressed that she was the rule,[10] the life, and the teaching of the holy apostles. The sixth expressed that through her, God gave strength and constancy to the holy martyrs. The seventh expressed the piety of the confessors, which is the confessors' special virtue, through which they are rewarded abundantly through her intercession.

Chapter 14. Regarding the Saints' Closeness to God

The eighth expressed the chastity of virgins, because she was the first founder of the institution of virginity and had a copious crowd following her in the resolution towards a virginal life. And she said that virgins are closest to God. And she said that other saints who founded and instituted new ways of holiness such as Blessed Benedict, Blessed Bernard, Blessed Francis, Blessed Augustine and Blessed Dominic are in glory before other saints.[11] The ninth star expressed the beneficence that she showed toward sinners; and this star circled in the crown whereas the others were fixed stars. The tenth [represented] grace and the increase of grace, which the just receive through her. And therefore she said that she is like a canal or aqueduct, through which God flows into the elect, even in the fatherland. The eleventh is the authority and power according to the right of the mother to offer benefits before all other saints. The twelfth expressed the help given to those in purgatory, for whenever Masses and church services are celebrated in her memory, she herself retrieves a number of souls from punishments.

Her cloak, made of the sun, is the brilliant light of the divinity with which she is covered as if with a coat. That is, she herself is more translucent and is more permeated with divine light, that is divinity,

---

10 *Regula.*

11 Given the tensions between Dominicans and Franciscans during Blannbekin's time, the list's inclusivity is noteworthy. In other chapters, however, Blannbekin and her confessor scribe reflect on the intense rivalry and competition between the new orders. See especially chapters 16, 18, 20, 92. For a fuller discussion, see Dinzelbacher, "Die Wiener Minoriten im ausgehenden 13. Jahrhundert nach dem Urteil der zeitgenössischen Begine Agnes Blannbekin", in *Bettelorden und Stadt. Bettelorden und städtisches Leben im Mittelalter und in der Neuzeit*, edited by Dieter Berg (Werl: Dietrich Coelde Verlag, 1992), 181–91.

than all the saints. For this reason, the moon is under her feet. The light of the moon means that as the moon is inferior to the sun, so all brilliance of light emanating from the saints is inferior to the light and brilliance of the glorified Virgin.

Chapter 15. Regarding Angels

Regarding the blessed angels, she said that they exist without a body and are in God. As a rose, when put in front of a mirror, appears in the mirror, so are angels in the mirror of God. Having true being and true life, they burn in divine love, some more so than others, and they praise God and they see God; in this they experience the greatest joy.

They derive other joys from caring for our salvation by being solicitous of us. And since it brings honor to God and progress in salvation for us, they rejoice. They are such friends of the human species that they all would be prepared and willing to descend upon earth for the sake of just one soul so that it would not perish. And she said that although the angels are very close to God and burn in love, the love of many saints is stronger and therefore more precious, because the saints advance in the love of God by way of many difficulties and struggles.

Chapter 16. Regarding the Preeminence of the Apostles before All Other Saints

She said that the holy apostles are preeminent before all other saints with the exception of John the Baptist and Blessed Moses. And she gave as a reason that the Lord was close to them in life and spoke with them and that they were ablaze in love incessantly due to their life together and due to those conversations.

Chapter 17. Regarding Saint Paul

She said about Saint Paul that he would be the most significant among the apostles except for three, Blessed Peter, Blessed John the Evangelist, and Blessed Bartholomew, because Blessed Bartholomew had suffered for so long and so bitterly in the most passionate love of Christ.

Chapter 18. Regarding Francis

She said about Blessed Francis that he would be greatest in God's view except for the apostles, Blessed John the Baptist, and Blessed Moses. She said that Blessed Francis loved God earnestly and with the strongest and most passionate love, and that the soul of Blessed Francis has those small sacred signs because he burned most intensely in the love of Christ and within the soul; and therefore they appeared visibly on the body. And she said that the saints rejoice greatly about this, because someone was found among them in whom those sacred wounds of Christ were rekindled with light.[12]

Chapter 19. Regarding the Light that Emanates from the Wounds of Christ

She said that the light emanating from the wounds of Christ reflects so strongly from the stigmata of Blessed Francis and brings them iridescence such as the sun brings to the moon that the divine court rejoices over it.

Chapter 20. Regarding Blessed Bernard, Blessed Dominic, Blessed Nicholas, Blessed Augustine, Blessed Gregory and Saint Ambrose, Brother Berthold of Regensburg and Blessed Jerome

She said about Blessed Bernard, Blessed Dominic, and Blessed Nicholas that they are comparable to Blessed John the Evangelist in that they loved God with a most tender and sweet love and that they are the most excellent saints in heaven.

She said about Blessed Augustine that he is the greatest light before God and that he truly understood the Most Blessed Trinity, because he used his mind[13] and refined his intellect with such faith and love in [his] tractates on the holy trinity.

She said about Blessed Gregory that he might be the most beloved saint and that his soul, like Saint Stephen's, was a vessel filled with the Holy Spirit and the love of the spirit of the saints. Therefore he has influence and the signs of love in the fatherland.

She said that each one of the saints was glorified in the fatherland in the same fashion as he was given grace on his particular path [in life]. She said about Saint Ambrose that he was greatly glorified, because he loved justice so zealously. And she added that Brother Berthold of Regensburg was not less than he due to the grace of his teachings, because he taught and because he was austere toward

---

12 On St. Francis and his stigmata, see the overview in McGinn, *The Flowering of Mysticism: Men and Women in the New Mysticism (1200–1350)* (New York: Crossroad, 1998), especially pp. 59–64.

13 *Ingenium.*

himself.[14] She said that conducting one's life with austerity was meritorious before God. Regarding Blessed Jerome, she said that he was marked with divine light because he illuminated sacred scripture with such erudition.

Chapter 21. Regarding the Voice of Praise in the Fatherland

She said that a most sweet voice of praise existed in the homeland so that the song of just one angel would delight all [members] of the heavenly court, even if others were silent. And all the angels would sing with this voice as well as the souls of the elect, except for those entangled in grave sins, who had postponed penitence until the end of life. They died in this state, yet not without remorse, and they were gravely punished in the fire of purgatory. These people did not have the voice of praise. And the little children, who had not yet accumulated any merit, did not have the voice of praise either. However, the little children who suffered much illness – some children of two or three years of age and thereabouts – those have the voice of praise. As she said, to suffer in faith is very meritorious before God.[15]

Chapter 22. Regarding Diverse Singing Voices in the Homeland

She also said that not all sing with one voice in the homeland, but intone several voices and melodies, and some sounded sweeter than others according to their greater merit before God.

[14] Berthold of Regensburg was perhaps the most important German preacher in the thirteenth century; his close companion, the Franciscan David of Augsburg, might have influenced Franciscan spirituality as taught in Vienna, especially in his emphasis on the interior and exterior person, the importance of prayer and asceticism, and the union with God as an act of grace. See the discussion of David's spirituality in McGinn, *The Flowering of Mysticism*, chapter 3.

[15] This is a comforting view on the status of children who died in infancy. On the issue of children and female concern for them, see Clarissa Atkinson, *The Oldest Vocation: Christian Motherhood in the Middle Ages* (Ithaca: Cornell University Press, 1991), and more recently, Barbara Newman, *From Virile Woman to WomanChrist: Studies in Medieval Religion and Literature* (Philadelphia: University of Pennsylvania Press, 1995), chapter 3.

Chapter 23. Regarding the Voices of an Angel and their Pleasures, that is of the Angels and the Souls of the Blessed, and their Motion

The voice of those who praise and jubilate does not use words but is nonetheless intelligible to the intellect; and it was so sweet and so joyful that if only one angelic voice sounded on the earth, the whole world would exult. She said that the spirits of angels and blessed souls experience pleasure in indescribable delight, channeled into them by God, so that their desire is continually renewed and they always experience new delight, without any change or newness occurring around the Divine. She herself does not know whether this rapture happened in the body or outside the body.

I asked her whether the Blessed Souls move from one place to another. She answered, "No". She said that she knew most certainly that if she could have been able to sing, the soul's joy would have become so great that her body would have died, because that force or pact which obligates the body to be at the service of the soul would have been completely debilitated.

I asked her whether she drew anything from such contemplation and brought it [back] with her. Devoutly and covered in tears, she humbly responded, "Yes", because throughout her life, she has had many visitations from the Holy Spirit, consolations and revelations from the Lord. Yet she always shuddered with a certain fear and suspicion, because in her estimation she was unworthy and even ungrateful for so many and such great gifts. Therefore she often feared that the Lord would abandon or punish her gravely. But after this miraculous revelation, this fear was taken from her in such a way that when this fear touched her even only lightly, she would quickly feel in her soul a certain spiritual touch, comforting her as if to say, "Do not fear anything!" And she said that in this consolation the loving kindness of God became a sweetness in her soul that flowed into her exterior senses and expanded through her whole body and that she felt warmth around her heart.

In any case, I believe that the Holy Spirit then spreads in her heart. She also said that throughout her life, however much she blazed in a great desire for the body of the Lord, when she ought to have taken communion, a certain fear had always invaded her so that her very limbs shook and her teeth clattered until she received communion. After that particular revelation, such trembling had left her.

She also said that after this visitation and revelation, she had revelations from God and spiritual consolations more frequently, such that they occurred at least once during a natural day. She also said that previously she had often had revelations of the Lord, but they suddenly escaped her memory, [lapses] that I also have experienced with her. After this vision, however, whenever she wishes, she can remember whatever was revealed to her. She also said that before, she enjoyed the exterior reality of beautiful altar ornaments and paraments and statues or images of the saints, because she drew much spiritual consolation from them. Since that vision, however, she cares less [about them] due to the greater consolation, which she receives internally from that which she sees in the spirit. She says indeed that when she wishes to make time for contemplation, she directs her concentration toward whatever she wills from those things that are revealed to her in a vision from the Lord. The Lord is so generous and prompt that He quickly infuses her with the blessing of His sweetness as if someone who gently knocks at a door is immediately invited to enter. And it happens often that she is carried off into an ecstasy and with exterior senses dulled, her heart is on guard internally, and a vision of those things is given to her, which she had concentrated upon at the beginning of her contemplation. Sometimes something new and not previously seen will be revealed in such a vision. But this ecstasy happens suddenly. All that is said above belongs to one single vision.

Chapter 24. Regarding the Five Types of Works for Human Beings

She also saw another vision in the spirit. And behold, Lord Jesus appeared dressed in a dalmatica of a very brilliant heavenly color and engaged incessantly in five different actions among human beings. He painted some, dressed others, some He increased, others He decreased, some He fed. He performed these works one at a time, first in one human being so that it appeared that He only painted one person, only clad one person, and so on with each one. Then He performed these tasks for an infinite multitude of human beings; and among some He only performed one work, among others two, or several, that is, sometimes He only painted, sometimes He painted and clad, and similarly among the others. It was given to her to understand this vision. The painting symbolizes the rejuvenation of the mind. As a painter renews an old sculpture by covering it with colors, so Christ [renews] the minds of the sinners. The clothing symbolizes virtuous and strenuous labors, that is abstinence, vigils and similar practices. For this reason, she told me that a certain noble woman, whom I knew, who lived in great sanctity, appeared dressed in ivory clothing and had eyes like the flames of fire, and the pieces of clothing with which the Lord dressed her were many-colored and diverse. It symbolizes the increase and the addition of grace that He bestowed on some people much like someone adds to an ingot of gold another lump of gold by melting them together.

But when He diminishes some human beings it symbolizes the withdrawal of grace from certain people because of their indolence and neglect. That He also fed some symbolizes the spiritual food of internal consolation. Truly, the Lord engaged in these five labors continually. When I heard this, a certain word of the Savior came into my memory: "My Father worked until now, and now I work."[16]

She saw many human beings she had known previously in this vision and recognized what the Lord worked in them. Yet the fact that the Lord first labored only in one person and then in many means that the Lord is as concerned about the salvation of one as of many. Therefore, if there were only one person in the world, He would work for the salvation of one with such charity, such fidelity and concern as He is now working for the salvation of many.

Chapter 25. Regarding the Three Heavens

On the day of St. Nicholas, when she had received communion of the body of the Lord and wished to dedicate herself to contemplation, suddenly in the same church, the hand of the Lord came over her. And Christ appeared to her, dressed in a bishop's vestments, and showed her three heavens. The first was of the Most Blessed Trinity. When He showed her this, such an immense light burst forth, indeed unbearable to her, and suddenly disappeared as if in the blink of an eye. Light remained, however, in which Christ appeared to her. All apparitions or revelations indeed happened to her in a pleasurable light.

The second heaven was the dwelling of the Blessed. The third heaven was the just and holy soul while still existing in the body. And she heard a voice telling her, "All joy that you have seen, and the glory of the saints are like a drop of water in comparison to the ocean. So is all that you have seen in comparison to that which you have not yet seen. And as a drop is in relation to the ocean, so is all joy which all have who are in heaven, in comparison with God's joy, which He has always enjoyed within Himself and enjoys now. He

---

16 See John 5:17–18.

delights not at all less in the third heaven, that is in the holy soul, which is still surrounded by so many weaknesses and nonetheless loves God so much and strives to please God with all her strength."

Chapter 26. Regarding Three Places, that is the Kitchen, the Pharmacy, and the Shop of God, or Rather, Christ

In the same vision, Christ appeared to her clad in a bishop's vestments, all except for the chasuble. The paraments had the color of heaven, and the miter shone with gold and precious stones. And three sites and a great multitude of people surrounded Him as if it were the whole world. He had a kitchen at one place, where He alone prepared food. In another area, He had a pharmacy with aromatic herbs, where He alone prepared medicines.[17] At the third location, He had a store where He, like a shopkeeper, displayed a diversity of goods.

And people went to all three places to get something from what was available. So they went to the kitchen for food, to the pharmacy for medicines, and to the store for merchandise. And some would be completely rejected from there, and it was forbidden that they should receive anything. Others were set some limits, and so they did not receive immediately what they desired. Others received immediately and without difficulty what they needed. She who saw this vision also understood its meaning.

Chapter 27. Regarding the Foods of the Kitchen

Christ prepared the dishes in the kitchen. The first dish was no doubt made from warm and aromatic specialties and represents devout remembrance, with great compassion, for the passion of Christ. As she said, there the soul is kindled and ignited. In this flaring up of compassion, the soul receives a certain divine likeness.

The second dish seemed to have been made from milk, that is the milk of almonds, and it represents sorrow and compassion for the sins of our neighbors, since milk represents a certain sweetness of compassion.

The third dish seemed to have been made of butter, which in itself is a sweet food and refines and augments the taste of other foods. And it signifies prayer, which in itself is sweet and good for everything.

---

[17] For a discussion of the venerable theme of Christ as healer, see Margot Schmidt, *Mechthild of Magdeburg. Das fliessende Licht der Gottheit* (Stuttgart and Bad Cannstatt: Frommann-Holzboog, 1995), 397–400.

Christ also prepared brine made of vinegar, which represents the fear of God, and also of strong herbs, which symbolize the manifold regeneration of grace in the devout soul, and of aromatic powders, and these signify divine consolation.

Chapter 28. Regarding the Apothecary's Medicinals

In the second location, He had an apothecary with medicines, which He Himself had prepared. And there were two kinds; some indeed promoted spiritual health, which made them three. He had and gave to some a sleep-inducing potion, which symbolizes the grace of the Holy Spirit. When drunk, a person falls asleep to the world because of contempt [for the world] so that he does not care about worldly matters, much like somebody asleep with numbed senses does not feel anything.

Secondly, He had a strengthening remedy, and it represents the invigoration of good will and the execution of a virtuous deed which the Lord guides. Thirdly, He had and administered a certain sweet and delightful powder, which can be taken at any hour, and it symbolizes the tasting of devotion through which God can be tasted at all times.

There were also many sick with different kind of illnesses, all of whom found a suitable remedy. And I will name only three types of illness so as to avoid tedium: there appeared some lepers, some with dropsy, and some that were blind. And it was made apparent that the lepers represented those who indulge in debauchery, those with dropsy, avaricious people, and the blind, people full of pride.

Against leprosy, He administered different types of water extracted from diverse plants through the strength of fire and with the help of words [incantations], such as roses, violets and the like. They symbolize the various types of confusion into which those who are lascivious fall and through which they are called back and cured of the leprosy of debauchery. Against dropsy, that is avarice, He gave a loosening remedy, and it represents the damage of things and the loss of temporary goods and so unhappiness, through which the greedy are frequently cured. Against blindness, that is pride, He offered a desiccating paste, which symbolizes the anguish of illnesses and adversities, through which pride is often healed.

Chapter 29. Regarding the Merchandise of Christ's Shop

In the third place was also a shop with various merchandise of which I will name a few items. There was gold, which symbolizes divine love. There were precious stones and gems, which represent the perfection of divine love. There was also jewelry such as rings and similar trinkets, which represent the anguish that the Lord gives to those who are His in this world. There were precious clothes, and two types of clothing, that is coats and tunics. There were two types of cloaks, namely a white and shiny coat, which symbolizes the example of a holy life, and there was also a red cloak. It signifies the disgrace and contempt through which a guiltless person is sometimes humiliated and vilified by others. These are [caused by] opprobrium and calumnies as had been said to the Lord, "With Beelzebub, the prince of demons, He drives out demons."[18]

And the Lord dressed others in that cloak only temporarily and did not give it away, because He will eventually liberate human beings [from such suffering]. There were also two types of tunic, one green, the other multi-colored. The first symbolizes the harshness of life and the other the variety of virtues. Because some that came were completely rejected and barred from everything, as told above, it represents those who are unworthy of God's grace because of their exceeding guilt. But to others not everything was denied, and they were led into [the store] after a delay. This represents those who are not worthy of God's grace now, but will be worthy in the future in a state of penitence. However, others immediately received what they wished. It represents those who, already [well] ordered, reach out for God's grace. And she said that most of those rejected empty-handed were the arrogant type of sinners.

Chapter 30. Regarding the Weaknesses and Sins of Individual Persons

In the fifth night of the Lord's nativity, the Lord honored her by granting her a new type of visitation. In the middle of the night and all alone in her prayer cell, she offered the hours of Matins to God as was her custom. She felt and she heard within her chest a serene voice, mild and sweet. As the voice began, she felt a certain sweetness rise up high, and in that sweetness she heard a voice using words and calling her by her name. This voice, however, began to list the weaknesses and the sins of individual persons, sometimes of people

---

18 See Matthew 12:24.

who took religious vows, sometimes of lay people, sometimes of princes, sometimes of barons. Horrified, she herself refused to listen and continued to read Matins. And although it was horrible to her to hear that, she nonetheless felt in her soul a not insignificant sweetness. She wondered greatly from where this voice came, and why, if it stemmed from God, He would reveal to her such things. She said nothing, and contemplated it.

And afterwards, she was taught in another revelation described below that the Lord did this so that she would co-suffer with the Lord the great injuries and ingratitude toward Him from those to whom He had granted so many favors, and so that she herself, shaken as she was, deserved to hear something consoling. And that revelation which frightened her so lasted about as long as it took the friars to sing Matins.

Chapter 31. Regarding the Virtues and Merits of Many Persons

And again, the Lord called her by her name and enumerated the virtues and merits of many individual persons, some among the religious, some among the prelates, some among the laity, just as He had told her before about shortcomings. And when He commended the virtues of someone, He gave him a new name. He named and called someone "Bringer of Light", telling about his virtues. Another He named "Aurora", and another He called "Planet and Star which Circles and Shines with the Sun". [Yet] another He called "Perfect Praise of God"; another He called "Voice in which I Praise Myself Perpetually". Another He called "Light, Brightened by the Sun of Divinity and Light in which I Shine to Myself". Another He called "Light Shining in Dark Clouds"; another, "Steward of the Lord". Another He named "Peace of God"; another He called "Light which I Myself Lightened". Another person He called "Spirit of My Spirit, that is Spirit Enlivened by My Spirit and Having from My Spirit Whatever it has". Another He called "Praise which Carries Me Continually". Another He called "Praise in which I Please Myself well". Another He called "Voice which Praises Me Continually". Another He called "Voice of Grace to which I will Add Grace". Another He called "Sweet Sound, which Praises Me often". Another He called "Conflict", that is a war,[19] "in which I Conduct Myself

---

[19] In a few places throughout the text, Middle High German words are inserted. Here, the Latin *contentio* is explained with the German *einen chriek*, a war. Chapter 30 is reminiscent of Hadewijch's list of the 86 perfect, which she added to her vision no. 13. Both lists indicate informal networks and spiritual "rating systems" among

Honorably". Another He called "Light, which is Often Extinguished and Often Rekindled". Another He called "Lamp which Shines Continually". Another He called "A Sweet Flute of My Praise, but a Humble Fruit in Itself". Another He called "Grace with Grace". Another He called "Perfect Joy" and another "Life in the Lord": Another He called "Spirit in which I am Pleased with Myself", another "Light that Shines for Me before My Father", another "Continually Living Justice".

*   *   *20

Chapter 34. Regarding a Voice which Expressed Praise of the Savior in Five Ways

At the Feast of the Lord's Circumcision, when she had taken communion, she felt and heard within a voice expressing itself neither verbally nor with syllables, but yet praising God.[21] She realized also that it was the celestial voice which she had heard in the rapture of the first vision of this little book, and understood in this voice the fivefold praise of the Savior. The first praise occurred because God became a human being and because of all that He achieved for human beings in [His] humanity; the second because of the effects of grace through which He labors continually within the just; the third because of the patient expectation with which He expects sinners; the fourth because of the many benefits offered to sinners, so that He may win them for Himself and through which He calls them to Himself; the fifth because He gives Himself to a human being.

And when she heard this, she reflected [upon this] in her thoughts and spoke, "O Lord, whatever it was and wherever it may have come,

medieval spiritual seekers. How these lists were used is difficult to determine. Hadewijch notes at the end of hers, "I do not know what you can make of all these people as their lives are unknown to you and in what marvelous way they have arrived at this perfection or shall arrive at it." See Helen Rolfson, "Hadewijch of Antwerp, *The List of the Perfect*", *Vox Benedictina* 5:4 (1988): 277–88.

20   Chapters 32 and 33 discuss the proper attitude of priests during Mass. Agnes is not mentioned in the chapters.

21   The motif of "mystical unsaying" (Michael Sells) or mystical knowledge beyond human language has been systematically explored as early as Pseudo-Dionysius (end of the fifth century CE) and is usually subsumed under the technical term of *via negativa*. It seems to be woven into Agnes's spirituality experientially and, as it were, situationally rather than systematically. See Michael Sells, *Mystical Languages of Unsaying* (Chicago: University of Chicago Press, 1994).

what I have heard yesterday, I know that what I am hearing now, cannot but be from You, because I still feel bodily and spiritually the influence of Your consolation with which You used to comfort me in the reception of Your Holy Body. For that reason, deception can not be the case here." While she was thinking these words, she heard again a voice speaking to her: "You poor little one, what are you doubting, having so much evidence of the truth from Me? It is Me who speaks, who in the past spoke through the mouth of prophets. In the way I spoke with Moses in the thorn bush – and this occurred not because of any virtue on the part of the thorn bush – so it is my present what I speak to you and within you, not your virtue or merit."[22]

* * *[23]

Chapter 37. Regarding the Foreskin of Christ

On the feast day of the Circumcision, almost from her youth onwards, and fearfully because of great and heartfelt compassion, this person always used to cry over the blood Christ deigned to shed so early at the beginning of His childhood. And this was what she did when the already mentioned revelation occurred, when she received communion on the feast day of the Circumcision.

Crying and with compassion, she began to think about the foreskin of Christ, where it may be located [after the Resurrection]. And behold, soon she felt with the greatest sweetness on her tongue a little piece of skin alike the skin in an egg, which she swallowed. After she had swallowed it, she again felt the little skin on her tongue with sweetness as before, and again she swallowed it. And this happened to her about a hundred times. And when she felt it so frequently, she was tempted to touch it with her finger. And when she wanted to do so, that little skin went down her throat on its own. And it was told to her that the foreskin was resurrected with the Lord on the day of resurrection. And so great was the sweetness of tasting that little skin that she felt in all [her] limbs and parts of the limbs a sweet transformation. During this revelation, she was so filled with light within that she could gaze at herself completely [as in a reflection].

---

22 This dialogue repeats a theme in Blannbekin's confessor scribe's prologue to the visions.

23 Chapters 35 and 36 discuss the nature of those taking communion.

And because it is good to hide God's sacrament, this person was afraid to share this divinely inspired revelation with me, her unworthy confessor, and she often resolved in her mind to not tell me anything further of it. And whenever she firmly determined [this], she began to get sick, so that she could not keep silent, since God wanted it [i.e. sharing her vision].

I, on the other hand, was really very comforted that the Lord deigned to show Himself to a human being in such a way, and greatly desired to hear [about it]. And she herself told me that one day, when she wanted to receive communion and the time had passed [and] she gave up hope of receiving communion anywhere, she herself asked the Lord in her heart and said, "Lord, if it is Your will that I shall tell the friar, my confessor, what You deigned to reveal to me, then provide me with the communion of Your sacred body today, and this shall be a sign to me."

And then she went to a certain monastery, and after the public Mass, the chaplain of that community arrived, who for some reason had neglected to say Mass and officiated much later than usual, and he gave her communion of the Body of the Lord.

Chapter 38. Regarding Three Presents Promised to the Scribe of the Little Book

And soon afterwards in that place, the hand of the Lord came upon her, and among other matters, she learned during a revelation that the Lord promised me, the scribe of that which I learned from her, three things. First, that no temptation of any kind would overpower me; second, that the Lord wished to give me an increase of His grace; and third, that the Lord wished to give Himself to me as a reward. Likewise on the fourth day before the Lord's epiphany, when she was still afraid to reveal to me the Lord's visitations, she asked the Lord during Mass saying, "O Lord, if it pleases You that I reveal to my confessor that which You deign to show me, then give me as a sign and proof that I will feel the consolation which I felt from the little skin of your foreskin on the Day of Circumcision. If You will not give me that which you gave me then, it will be a sign that it does not please You. And I will rather leave the town than that I will tell him anything more."

And see how great is the goodness of God and His inexpressible miracles! And soon indeed she felt the little skin on her tongue with such sweetness that she felt a change in body and spirit as had happened to her on the Day of Circumcision. And although divinely comforted through so many indications, nonetheless she talked to me shyly and with fear, pursued by me with frequent questions.

Indeed, she believed herself to be completely unworthy of so many divine gifts and humbled herself with humility, because I was greatly consoled and comforted through her revelations, reminding myself of Blessed Gregory's text "The Human Mind" etc.[24]

Chapter 39. Regarding the Holiness of her Life, Namely, of the Virgin Who is the Topic of this Book

The fact that she served the Lord most devoutly from the beginning of her youth also proved to me the holiness of her life. When she was still a young girl, she never mingled with those who played games, but, while the other girls gathered for childish pleasures, she remained at home and worshipped God the Father in secret. As the Holy Spirit taught her, she began to afflict herself with miraculous abstinence, so that she, pretending to eat whatever was put before her, took it in a pious act of stealing and distributed it among the pious poor. And thus, forcefully subduing nature, she was tortured by such hunger that she often cried bitterly when alone. Beginning at the age of seven, she spent a good ten years of her life with such martyrdom of voluntary hunger for God's sake. For thirty years, she hardly ate any meat at meals. Every day except for Sundays, she fasted. She said that she never ate with the pleasure of tasting [the dish] and that she often cried, because she had to eat material [rather than spiritual] food. And because she had abstained with such austerity from the pleasures of the flesh since her youth, the Lord generously offered her spiritual delights, as will become obvious through numerous examples given below.

When she was eleven years old, she was inflamed with great devotion for the Body of the Lord [Eucharist]. When she received Him, she physically felt in her mouth an inexpressible sweetness, and as

---

24 Perhaps a reference to Gregory of Nyssa (d. 395), *De hominis opificio* (*Patrologia Graeca* 44: 125–256; Turnhout: Brepols, 1959). Certainly, Gregory's Neoplatonic emphasis on the possibility of experiential knowledge of God would form an appropriate theological context for and justification of Agnes's mystical experience. For a recent exploration of Gregory's mysticism in contemporary scholarship, see Martin Laird, "Gregory of Nyssa and the Mysticism of Darkness: A Reconsideration", *Journal of Religion* 79:4 (1999): 592–616. Gregory's concept of *epektasis*, or the soul's advancement toward God, might be especially relevant to chapter 69.

she recounted, all earthly sweetness was in comparison to this sweetness as vinegar is in comparison to honey.

Then she assumed that all who took communion would feel such sweetness. And when she heard that some priests gave themselves to carnal lust, she wondered how they could disdain such sweetness and enjoy such filth.

She hastened all the more quickly to become a Beguine so that she could take communion more frequently. When she takes communion, she feels this sweetness and pleasantness of taste, but not only has she experienced the sweetness of the bodily sense of taste, but also a miraculous spiritual sweetness in the soul. I, however, was reminded of that promise of the Lord in the Apocalypse, "I will give hidden manna to the winner",[25] and of the words in Deuteronomy which were truly fulfilled in her, "He afflicted you with lack of food and gave you as food manna which you and your fathers did not know."[26]

Friar Otto of the Franciscan Order told me something similar. He said that when he was about eighteen years old, living a very simple life in his father's house and raised among simple and rural people in the countryside, he was forced to take communion at Easter. Until then still untouched by any mortal sin and without having undergone confession, he took communion in great simplicity [of mind]. And, amazing to say and greatly consoling to our faith, he immediately, upon receiving the Body of Christ in the mouth, tasted such sweetness and pleasantness that it surpassed the sweetness of honey and balm. And thinking that he always ought to feel such sweetness when he took communion, he anticipated with desire the Easter celebration of the following year to receive the Body of Christ again, but then he did not feel anything.

It is a great solace for our faith that this virgin, about whom I spoke above, not only physically feels a sweetness in her mouth similar to the one mentioned above during the hour of communion when she hears something Divine during Mass, but [experiences] an inexpressible sweetness of soul and heart as well. And if it happens that the Lord withholds such consolation from her – it happens rarely, yet sometimes it does – then she is extraordinarily desolate.

---

[25] See Revelation 2:17.
[26] See Deuteronomy 8:3; 16.

Chapter 40. Regarding this Virgin's Kisses of the Altar

There is yet another miraculous thing, not less than this. Motivated by devotion, this virgin was used to kissing those altars on which Mass was celebrated that day. And then she experienced such a fragrant scent, similar to a warm, sweetly smelling roll, but incomparably sweeter. And she said that once, in the evening, she again kissed the altar with the wish to be uplifted by this very sweet scent. Then she smelled it, but not as much as in the morning when Mass had just been celebrated. And what is very miraculous, she said, is that she once recognized through fragrance what friar had celebrated Mass there.

Chapter 41. Regarding a Certain Priest who had Deflowered a Virgin and in this State [of Sin] Celebrated Mass

She burned with great devotion for the Body of Christ – she took communion every week. For this reason, the Lord deigned to show her miraculous and great things about this sacrament. When she was still a young virgin of about sixteen years of age, news of something horrible happened to these pious ears: namely, that during one night, a priest deflowered a young virgin in the town where that virgin stayed. The following day, he celebrated Mass because of a funeral, which he had to perform. And since it was market day, there were only a few people present besides the pious Beguines. And since the crime was out in the open and known to all, they were horrified to listen to the Mass celebrated by that priest. And while everybody retreated, she [Agnes] said in great pain, "Today, I wish to be Mary Magdalene." And she asked the Lord, "Lord, I beg you that, if he is among the number of those who will be saved, you will permit him to take the Body of Christ."

And behold, after the Our Father during that Mass, she herself felt and truly had the host in the mouth and swallowed it with such sweetness as she was used to while taking communion. The priest, however, when it was his turn to receive the Body [of Christ], looked around at the altar as if he had lost something.

But some years later, it happened that the Lord struck that priest with epilepsy; having become so useless and unfit for the office of the priesthood and having become as good as deaf, he was thrown into such misery that together with other beggars he accepted alms at the doors. Through the compassion of the Lord who does not want anybody to perish, he became so devout and contrite that he spent the whole day praying in church. And although he could well have accepted a God-fearing sponsor who would have provided him with the daily necessities, he rejected this and rather chose to live in such poverty among people of such notoriety and to engage in such hard penance. In this way, he spent three and a half more years and ended life happily.

Chapter 42. Regarding the Elevation of the Host through Four Fingers, Four Images, and their Meaning

Most often, she fell in ecstasy during Mass, where secrets were revealed to her. One time during Mass, while in ecstasy, she saw the Lord's body elevated through four fingers/through four images. There appeared namely the Blessed Virgin who touched the host with one finger. Another was the image of the old Simon, also touching the host with one finger. There also appeared a cross with one finger. There also appeared a donkey with one hoof. And since those four, that is the Blessed Virgin, the Holy Cross, Holy Simon, and the donkey carried the Lord physically in the world, they carried him there mystically. And she said that these figures or images seemed to have life except for the cross. And it was given her to understand that these four fingers represent four types of human beings who take the Body of the Lord in communion. The finger of the Blessed Virgin symbolizes the officiating priest, because, as the Blessed Virgin brought the Savior physically into the world and presented him, so does the officiating priest bring him and other sacraments to the people. And this was the index finger of the right hand.

The finger of the Holy Cross symbolizes those who partake of the Body of the Lord with devoted memory of the Passion. And this was the thumb of said hand. The finger of Holy Simon was the index finger of the left hand and represents the simple-minded and those who have pious desire for Christ. The fourth finger was the thumb of the left hand [hoof] that the donkey extended. It represents the sinners who do not grasp the fruit or the grace of the Sacrament.

*   *   *27

Chapter 44. Regarding an Unconscious Reverence Shown to a Basement by Bowing [in Front of it]

Another increase in our faith happened, most worthy of every veneration. This devout maidservant of Christ, visiting churches because of a sermon or indulgence or out of devotion, often passed the house

---

27 Chapter 43 discusses a corrupt priest.

of a certain merchant, and whenever she walked by, unconsciously showed reverence to the basement by bowing. This was noticed by devout, attentive persons who accompanied her; in speaking to her about it, they all made jokes about it. She, however, was unable to stop this kind of veneration which she did not engage in of her own will, but because of the instigation by the Holy Spirit, as became clear at the end.

Namely, when she had completed [her veneration] properly, priests from the parish came with devotion, hymns and songs, with banners and a procession of clerics and the people to carry away the Body of the Lord [the host] that a certain witch had hidden in a wine vessel for her own profit [in the aforementioned basement]. Driven by remorse, the woman, a witch, confessed this to a priest, and, to save her person, secretly disappeared. When the persons who previously laughed saw this, they all together praised the Lord in admiration.

Chapter 45. Regarding the Sparks which Jumped from the Host into the Mouth of the Priest

When she once heard Mass as she had always been accustomed to, with great faith and devotion, she saw in a physical vision that individual sparks of fire jumped from one part of the host into the mouth of the priest.

*   *   *28

Chapters 47, 48, 49, and 50. Regarding the Baptism of Christ, the Father, the Son, the Holy Spirit and Several Types of Human Beings, in Regard to whom the Holy Spirit Seems to be Active or is Active.

On the Octave of the Epiphany, when she had been to communion, all of the body began to be infused with great heat, which was not burning, but sweet, and soon she was completely encompassed in the spirit as well as interiorily with a divine light. She recognized, understood and saw [but] did not hear a physical voice. And it was revealed to her that in Christ, baptism was enacted tangibly, and that the Blessed Trinity became manifest, that is the Father in the voice, the Son in the flesh, the Holy Spirit in the dove, and in the Jordan the

---

28 Chapter 46 describes the spiritual meaning of priestly garments and reiterates that Agnes feels great sweetness during Mass, which revives and renews her.

baptized Christ. In such a way all of this happens spiritually in the souls of the devout: the Father manifests Himself in the voice when devout souls, with their spirit raised into the Divine, are instructed internally in Divine secrets either through insight or sometimes through a voice as disclosed above. The Son manifests Himself with love. And she said that the river Jordan appeared flowing from a mountain, and that this river was collected from the tears of love and devotion shed by holy souls.

And Christ appeared in such immense light as [described] above in the first vision, that is in heavenly light. And He appeared naked in that river and He enjoyed Himself more in that Jordan than in the physical Jordan. And the body of Christ appeared to be as translucent as a crystal in a sunbeam, and above Christ was a great white mountain which seemed to press down upon Him; and He was stronger [because of it]. It symbolizes the love which Christ had and still has for us that conquers Him and presses down on Him until death, with such force that during His dying, no blood remained in Him.

And that mountain, that is the magnitude of love, still presses down upon Him so that charisms of grace flow from it to those who venerate His Passion. Likewise, another mountain appeared above Him, on which many human beings appeared spread out every-where and holding on to the mountain. This mountain, as she understood it, represents the love with which human beings love Christ. The human beings who appeared there indeed symbolize those who have the love of Christ. But that some pulled the mountain so powerfully toward themselves represents those who are so powerful in the love of Christ that they exult over all virtues and good deeds of those around them and over the honor which is bestowed upon God and those around them. And they appropriate to them-selves the merits of the others by rejoicing over the good of others as if over their own.

There also appeared a dove, that is the Holy Spirit in a dove, and around it a multitude of human beings. This dove also sat on the heads of some, pulled the hair off the heads of others, lightly stuck its little beak into the mouth of others as if to kiss. Others it gave to eat, some it gave to drink, into others it blew fire, some it gave of its feathers, and others it covered with its wings as if embracing them.

That the Holy Spirit in the shape of a dove sat on the heads of some signifies that the Holy Spirit elevates the minds of those persons to heavenly things. But that it pulls hairs from some people symbolizes afflictions and tribulations, which humble their hearts. That it lightly stuck its little beak into the mouths of others as if to kiss [them] represents the sweetness of the Holy Spirit's consolations. That it fed some represents the Holy Spirit's offering of strength. That it gave others to drink symbolizes the infusion of grace transmitted through sermon and prayer. That it blew fire into some people signifies the kindling of charitable love. That it gave others of its feathers represents the renewal of grace. That it covered some with its wings as if embracing them symbolizes rapture in ecstasy. The dove accomplished all this.

*   *   *29

Chapter 54. Regarding the Blessed Virgin's Birthing and the Nativity of Christ

On the feast day of the Conversion of St. Paul, this virgin went to communion in a sad and desolate mood, because she was not prepared in such a way as she wished. As soon as she had swallowed the sacred communion, spiritual joy and a gentleness of spirit replaced this jolt of sadness. And it seemed to her that she was changed and renewed in body and spirit. And when she sat down again, the hand of God came over her and in the previous[ly described] light a young virgin with a beautiful face appeared to her. She was about thirteen years of age.

And she saw that suddenly, almost in an instant, a male child was formed in her uterus from the blood around her heart. He was immediately fully developed in all his body parts. Then she saw how the child was born by the Virgin and then how it lay naked in the mother's lap, suckling [her] breasts and wrapped in the mother's headscarf. Yet the child's eyes glimmered like sparkling stars. Then she saw the child wrapped and swaddled in fabrics and nothing remained naked except for the face. And she saw him lying on straw in the manger. The ox and the donkey stood not above, but next to the manger. In this the Lord honored her, showing her the mystery of the incarnation and the nativity.

---

29 Chapter 51 describes how Christ encourages a priest. Chapters 52 and 53 catalogue different types of religious.

Chapter 55. Regarding the Mystery of the Passion and the Death of the Lord

Then He honored her by showing her the mystery of the passion and death as follows. She saw a young adult, fully naked except that a linen cloth was tightly wrapped around His body. That linen cloth was drenched in blood. She also saw how that man was nailed on a cross. The cross, however, did not stand up, but was laid upon the ground along its length and on it the young man was placed. And first the right hand was fixed on the cross, then the left hand, then the feet were stretched and, one put above the other, they were transfixed with one nail. The crown of thorns, by which He was taunted by those who crucified Him, pushed so hard on His head that the tips of the spines penetrated into His brain, because it moved somewhat while the cross was being carried. And [while lying] on the ground, He was transfixed on the cross; with the cross put upright, and while hanging on the cross, He searched for relief from one nail to the other where He could bear it more easily. The lance, piercing Him from the left side to the right side, was plunged into His heart. Thirst affected Him so very strongly that a most bitter potion was given Him. He cried such bitter and boiling hot tears that His cheeks seemed skinned, and with a powerful scream He expired.

Chapter 56. Regarding the Lord's Grave and its Meaning

Then she saw how He was taken down from the cross and wrapped in white linen and put into the grave and a stone was rolled over from nearby. And she heard a voice saying to her, "This grave symbolizes the human heart, where the Lord wishes to be buried through love and devout memory in the same way in which Joseph buried Him with a great feeling of love in His grave. The stone, which completely covered the Lord in the grave symbolizes a spiritual covering, because we must not divulge the gifts of God, the Divine visitations, consolations, revelations to the outside among the people, nor display the holiness of a life except in so much as is expedient for the good example and the edification of those around us [in order] to show bright examples through its [good] works. It is also necessary for us ourselves to be covered and concealed so that we esteem ourselves to be nothing in all that God works in us."

She was also told that the Lord visited six beds and [briefly] rested in each because in the seventh bed He would find a [permanent] place of rest there.

Chapters 57, 58, and 59. Regarding Christ's Visit of the Six Beds, the Four-fold Death of Christ on the Cross, and the Many Daily Uses of the Body of Christ on the Altar

The first bed was the Virgin's womb, to which He came from God's heart, drawn by great love. And as she heard this, she began to hesitate and to think by herself about the Father's heart, [and] in which manner the Father would have a heart. And it was told to her and explained, "The Father's heart is the will, therefore it follows that He came from the heart of the Father, that is from the will of the Father." The second bed was the Virgin's lap, in which He rested in human frailty, suckling His mother's breasts. The third bed was the manger, in which He rested with great humility. The fourth bed was the cross, on which He rested for the redemption and salvation of human beings. His rest, however, consisted of leaning upon and shifting from one nail to the other.

It was also said to her that the Savior endured a fourfold death on the cross. One was the death of the cross, that is the crucifixion. Another was the death of the lance, because, although He was already dead, nonetheless, the person who pierced His side intended His death. He would have died from that piercing had He still been alive then. The third was the death of the crown of thorns, whose spikes penetrated into His brain, so that each one of these punishments would have sufficed to induce death. The fourth death was a most bitter anguish of the heart, which was threefold. One vexation was in response to His mother's suffering. Secondly, the Lord was distressed that His passion would have had to be in vain in so many instances. The third affliction was over the ridicule extended toward Him.

The fifth bed was the grave. The sixth bed was the altar, where the living and true body of God is sacrificed for a manifold daily use. The first use is the remittance of sins, the second the memory of the passion, the third the increase of our virtues, the fourth the victory over temptations, the fifth the perfection of our life, and the sixth is the reward before the sight of the Father.

The seventh bed is the human heart. And it was said to her that the Lord visited the six previous beds because of this one, that is the human heart, so that He may rest there.

Chapter 60. Regarding the Six Virtues who Prepare the Lord's Bed

Six virtues were described to her there, with which the Lord's bed is prepared. The first is uprightness, the second humility, the third discipline, the fourth moderation, the fifth patience, the sixth love.

Chapter 61. Regarding the Six Virgins with Candles in their Hands, and their Exegetical Meaning, that is the Seven Virtues

It happened at the feast of the Purification of the Virgin Mary, while she took communion, that the Franciscan priest who administered the host to her touched her with the sacred host above her mouth. This caused her much fear since she believed that the host had broken and she felt great despair. Although feeling desolate, she continued to partake in the communion. Eventually, she also tasted the ineffable sweetness sensually and to no lesser degree in her heart as she was accustomed to. In the following night, however, when she had read Matins and wished to rest, the hand of the Lord came over her and look! Six most beautiful maidens stood before her, shimmering in inestimable brightness, who all carried large burning candles in their hands. The light of those candles was extraordinarily pure and very serene. They stood in joined pairs of two. And as they stood like this, they began to speak. The first said, "I am named Voluntary Poverty." Her comrade and companion said, "I am called Patience." The third said, "My name is the Desire to Suffer Much." Her colleague said, "I am named Obedience." In like manner, Voluntary Poverty said, "I search for God at all times." Patience responded to her, "Wherever I turn, I find Him." In the same manner, Desire to Suffer Much said, "I collect and make my own all good that is created in the Church." Then her companion, that is Obedience, said, "I am ready for every perfection."

When these four had finished their presentation, the last two companions spoke. And the first said, "My name is Prayer." The last one said, "I am called Love." In like manner, the virgin who is called Prayer said, "I have God always." Her companion, who is called Charity or Love,[30] responded well, saying, "Whatever you ask, I give you." And the one called Love added, "Why is it that she, the devout woman [Agnes] did not see the souls of the lesser just persons like Sister Gertrud, but only the major saints?" And she herself answered

---

30 Blannbekin and her scribe seem to use the Latin terms *caritas* and *amor* synonymously, as the above sentence indicates.

her own question, saying, "The reason is that only those were shown to her who were perfect in holiness when they were on the way and in this life. And whoever wishes to be perfect needs to have the six of us, and who lacks one of us, is not perfect in holiness."

And then this virgin who is called Charity tilted her candle toward her companion who was called Prayer. Receiving something like a burning spark from Charity's torch, she threw it away from herself onto the chest of this devout woman [Agnes] who heard and saw this. She soon felt the fire of devotion in her heart and the spirit of a miraculous sweetness in her chest.

Chapter 62. Regarding a Star in which Appeared a Very Beautiful Human Face

On the fourth day after Purification, when that small divine spark glowed in her chest (which the virgin named Prayer threw on her chest when she had received the spark from the burning candle, as it has been said in the previous vision), this virgin began to cry most bitterly because of her distance from the fatherland. And as she cried inconsolably, she looked through the small window and saw one of the larger stars, in which appeared the face of a most beautiful human being. Upon this sight, she began to cry even more abundantly and fervently. And as she cried, she fell into ecstasy and that same face appeared to her in whom and in whose light she saw everything that exists in heaven and on earth [as described] in the first great vision of this book.[31] But now she saw all of this more clearly, and more pronounced. She saw the glory and the renown and the honors of the glorified virgins and the holy angels and the apostles and the martyrs. And she saw the other great and perfect saints and recognized them according to their names as she saw them above. And later she saw a great crowd of people whom nobody could count, who were the holy and the elect, and they constituted such a multitude that she herself had to marvel.

Chapter 63. Regarding the Sonorous Voice in the Fatherland and Other Voices Expressing Threefold Praise, but without Voice

She also heard the most sweet and diverse voices of those who praised with a sonorous sound to be sure, not in words yet nonetheless meaningful to the intellect of the listeners as in the first vision.

[31] *Volumen.*

The voices of those who praised expressed a threefold reason for the praise. The first voice was, "Holy, Holy, Holy Are You, Creator."[32] And this voice sang in all angels and all saints in the fatherland, except for the recently baptized and thus departed children and those who were once in great sin and, although having departed with contrition, made no reparation through works. These did not possess the voice of praise, as has been also said in the first vision above. And in this praise everybody understood and recognized what he himself enjoyed of the benefit of creation. And they accompanied this praise with a zither with such desire as if, if it were possible, they wished to have [temporal rather than eternal?] time to praise. So great is their joy in this praise.

The second praise expresses the benefit of the redemption. And this praise was sung only by human beings, but the angels complemented this praise in a miraculous fashion.

The third praise expresses the benefit of the reward. And they felt inestimable joy over this, because it was He Himself, that is the God-Man, who remunerated them. And in this praise they recognized every reward with all who were to receive a reward, because God would reward every created being who would remain with them forever for their sake, not only the sun and the stars and the moon and the elements, but also even the smallest grain. This was for them the utter height of joy.

Chapter 64. Regarding a Voice that Said in Words, "I Am, I Am."

She also heard a strong voice speaking in words and with joy, "I Am, I Am." And this was the voice of the Lord Christ. In His Very Self resounded the Virgins and those without blemish vocally and tonally, but not with words. And no other saints sang this song.

*   *   *[33]

Chapter 66. Regarding Two Boastful Demons

There appeared also two demons behind the back of the friar confessor of this virgin while he was celebrating Mass. They appeared first after the elevation of the Eucharist. They were

---

32 See Revelation 4:8.
33 Chapter 65 describes the presence of angels during each Mass, who hover around the priest.

deformed in their faces and horrible in the disposition of their whole body, yet they did not invoke horror in this virgin. One of them stood to the right and the other to the left of the priest, a little bit behind him, and bowing before each other, they boasted that they instilled some fear in him who celebrated Mass and that they had created some kind of obstacle. That priest was in the habit of sometimes trembling too much before the fantasies of bad thoughts, although he suffered them completely against his own will.

Those demons disappeared, however, after the recitation of the Our Father. On the other hand, the holy angels remained there and officiated for as long as Mass was read. It also seemed to her that in that same place, she took the Body of the Lord from the hands of the officiating friar during communion. And when she came back to herself, she felt in her mouth and tasted physically the miraculous sweetness that she usually felt.

Chapter 67. Regarding the Voice Saying, "Do You Wish to Know what God is in the Soul and what He Works in the Soul?"

At another time, when she wished to devote herself to contemplation, she felt in the body and the chest a miraculous fire of devotion, so that the heat expanded physically throughout all of the body. And within her she heard a sweet and lovely voice as it was said above, and it said to her, "Do you wish to know what God is in the soul?" She, however, remained silent. And then said the voice, "God is a languid hunger in the soul, that is a desiring hunger[34] with a joyful heart."

She interpreted it as follows: "A languid hunger: that the soul hungers for God with the languor of love. A cheerful heart is a pure conscience." That voice also said, "Do you wish to know what God, who exists in the soul, works?" She, however, remained silent. And it said, "God who exists in the soul judges like a king in the kingdom, likewise He bestows magnificent gifts, likewise He conducts councils like a prelate with his own. Likewise, He shows himself to the bride as intimately as the bridegroom to the bride. Like a king, God judges homicides, that is mortal sins, with contrition and the disciplining of the sinners and through true penitence. Likewise He judges by restoring things which were taken away and badly ruined, that is He returns gifts of grace to the soul after she begins to submit

---

34 As in chapter 30, the scribe inserted a Middle High German expression, *ein seniger hunger*, next to the Latin *esuries languens*.

to the judgment of penitence. Likewise He judges by freeing pris-
oners unjustly imprisoned, that is the heart and the emotions of the
soul bound and fettered by illicit desires are freed through grace from
the yoke of servitude to carnal desires."

Chapter 68. Regarding the King who Offers Gifts to Three Types of Human Being, that is to Knights, to Minstrels, and to His Bride

The King also confers gifts to three types of human beings: knights,
minstrels, and His bride. The God-King is honored threefold in His
knights, namely in their dignity or nobility, in their strength, [and] in
their fidelity. Therefore God gives to His knights these three: the
dignity or nobility of the soul, which God gives and through which
He is honored in the soul, is purity and integrity.[35] The soul's
strength is that she resists temptation manfully. The soul's faithfulness toward God is love.

The minstrels are the five senses who praise, admonish, and exhil-
arate with new songs. They reprove by testifying to the soul's vices,
which they learned about through the five senses. They praise by
offering to the soul virtues that can be learned and which they
perceive and see in good persons. They sing enjoyable songs by
driving the soul to sigh devoutly through that which they perceive in
the external world.

God presents three gifts to the bride: first, divine revelations of
secrets to the degree as is beneficial for the soul. Second, He infuses
the soul's sense of taste with spiritual consolations and sweet delica-
cies. Third, He induces the soul to ardently hunger for God.

Chapter 69. Regarding God's Council in the Soul, with whom He Arrives at a Threefold Resolution

Likewise, God, who exists in the soul, discusses four issues with her.
First, He shows her the falsehoods and fickleness of the world.
Second, when the soul suffers and hurts because of injustices done to
God, [i.e.], that so many, forgetful of God's benefaction, dishonor
God through sins. They avert divine wrath that He would visit upon
them. Third, when the firstborn of God is offered to the people
through the hand of the priest. Fourth, He shows Himself to be close
to the soul, like a bridegroom to the bride, when [the bedroom] is
closed shut. The soul's little bedroom is closed shut, when the soul

---

[35] *Munditia.*

rests from all exterior works, even from good works, so much so that she cannot pray or do anything of the like, because through contemplation, she strives within herself toward God alone.

And when this happens in the soul, then God makes known to His bride, the soul, His most excellent will, that is the soul then begins to understand what pleases God the most and what He wills for her. By understanding this, the soul receives similitude with the Divine. Secondly, she begins to love God so much that she rejects all love and all that is lovable except that which will move her forward in the love of God. And through this love, the soul gains for herself whatever God has, and in the same way possesses with a sharing God whatever God has. Thirdly, the strength of good desire and good will is given to her, so that she intensely desires and burns for all that is good, and through this she buys herself whatever she wishes to have.

Chapter 70. Regarding Faith, Hope, and Charity

In this small bedroom, when Christ, the God as spouse, is going to enter the bridal bed of the spouse, Faith undresses Him, that is through Faith the bride deserves to see the bridegroom with His face revealed and without a veil. Hope places a footstool before the bridal bedstead so that He can enter with ease, when, however, nothing else weighs on the conscience. Love receives the bridegroom Himself in an embrace, and the bridegroom's Love in turn receives the soul in an embrace. And there happens such a union through the love of bridegroom and bride that the soul forgets herself. And above all of this is God's delight, and in this alone the soul responds to God's benefaction, that is that she loves with such love.

Chapter 71. Regarding the Five Types of Confessor who Hear People's Confessions

Taken into the spirit before the feast day of Palm Sunday, she saw five types of confessors who heard people's confession. Some had the heads of pigs and soiled snouts, others had the heads of dogs, others had a thoroughly frightening devilish disposition and faces like larvae, others had human faces, but splattered with blood, others had radiant human faces which were illumined by a certain divine light.

Therefore very surprised when she saw this, and wondering what it meant, she heard the voice within herself, as above, which said, "Those who have a pig's head and snout are confessors who hear confessions because of temporal profit and advantage. Those with a dog's head are confessors who hear confessions because of praise and vainglory and favors. In themselves unclean, they clean the wounds of others by licking and healing with their tongue. Those who have satanic shapes are apostates and also other sacrilegious persons whom God does not want you to know in order to spare you. Those who have human faces splattered with blood are confessors who violently force people to confess even that which they do not need to, and inquire about carnal matters for their own pleasure, and they are polluted within themselves. Those who have radiant human faces are confessors who hear confessions purely for God's sake and the salvation of souls."

Chapter 72. Regarding the Hands of the Priest, which Shone like the Serene Moon, and the Face of the Priest, which Was Resplendent like the Sun, and the Tent above the Body of the Lord and its Significance

Before Palm Sunday, when she attended a private Mass in the friars' church, where there were only a few people present, she went to a place after the elevation of the Body of the Lord where she could view the Body of the Lord on the altar. This was her habit, that whenever she could, she relished seeing the Body of the Lord treated with great desire and boundless faith. During the [chanting of the] canon therefore, a short while before the Our Father, she looked toward the altar, and behold, the hands of the officiating priest shone like the serene moon that appears during the day. And suddenly a stupor gripped her, not terrifying, but like a sweet appreciation. Also, the priest's face was resplendent like the sun, when it shines in a cloud or through a white cloud. And therefore she wondered about the source of this lunar and solar brilliance. And when she looked to the holy sacrament, she saw it shine like the sun in its strength. Then her bodily senses fell asleep, and she came into the spirit, and because she was held in great sweetness in those radiant lights which appeared to her fully embodied, she resisted being pulled into ecstasy from there, but she did not succeed.

And when she was in the spirit, the previously mentioned lights appeared inestimably large and imperceptible to bodily senses. Also, a tent or tabernacle appeared above the Body and Blood of the Lord, and it was inestimably refulgent, as if golden and yellow colors were carefully woven into it. An immense light also spread from the Body of the Lord. And in this light appeared a translucent image which turned now toward the priest, and now toward the holy sacrament.

And together with the priest, the image itself brought about all that is being done during Mass, in signs and in the breaking of the likeness [of Christ], and from that image, three beams reached toward the priest. The lunar light, which was directed toward the hands, signified priestly purity. In like manner, the solar radiance – and this was directed toward the face – signified purity of conscience. In like manner, the solar light, when it shines in the morning during sunrise – and this light penetrated into the heart – signifies the heart's desire for God.

Chapter 73. Regarding Many and Great Things which Happen under the Tent, that is the Dignity of the Priestly Office

The tent signifies the dignity of the priesthood, under which much that is great happens for the well-being of souls. Therefore, she saw under that tent an infinite multitude of humans, now being clothed, now being fed, now being painted, now being enlarged, just as she saw it also above in another vision, how all gems were formed of ivory and given to human beings.[36] Since [ivory] is by nature cool and gentle to the touch and noble, it signifies chastity, gentleness of spirit and soul, or the nobility of [good] manners. Then she thought quietly by herself, saying to herself [literally: within herself], "Oh God, why do You show me so many great things? Perhaps, because I am so small in faith and it is necessary that You strengthen me in faith in this manner, or that I am so prone to evil that I would fall if You would not take me by the hand." And she heard a voice within her saying, "Not so, but because of the great faith that you have in the sacred Eucharist."

Chapter 74. Regarding the Appropriate Time [with God], that is Fasting, and that it Is Better to Hear Confession than to Pray

On the feast of Palm Sunday, after she had taken communion and wished to make time for contemplation, a voice within her spoke, "Woe to those who neglect themselves now, because now is the right time and God is now more willing to give a favorable hearing in remembrance of the Savior's Passion, which is currently being commemorated, and because of the intensity of the prayers of the universal Church, which is at this time visited more often, and

---

36 The reference is probably to chapter 29, although ivory is not mentioned. A noble woman appears dressed in ivory clothing in chapter 24.

because of the devotion of human beings, because they are now more filled with devotion."

Then she thought quietly to herself, "Oh God, if only my confessor was free for prayer now!" For he was then occupied with hearing confessions and absolving sinners. And the voice said to her, "You little idiot, he could not pray any better now than he does hearing confessions and absolving sinners, because God the Father is powerfully present in the priest's word absolving the penitent and the Son in the hand of him who imposes penance, and what is missing, he supplements through his suffering. The Holy Spirit is at work there according to His goodness."

Chapter 75. Regarding the Plenitude of Maundy Thursday

On Maundy Thursday during Mass, she began to think again about the great demonstration of the Savior's grace, because He had instituted such an admirable sacrament on this day. And she heard the usual voice within her saying, "This is the day of the plenitude of grace and divine compassion, so that the just receive whatever they asked for." When she heard this, she thought, "Oh if I were among the number of those who are just." And she heard the voice within her saying to her, "You are of their number!" She, however, mistrusting her merits – she always greatly vilified herself in her own eyes – feared that she perhaps was not worthy to be given a favorable hearing together with the other just.

And she said, "Lord, if You honor me with accepting my prayers together with those others who are just, give me as a sign that this dust will settle which keeps your faithful from their devotional practices." Since an infinite number of people gathered in a crowd where the Lord Bishop of Passau reconciled the penitents, extremely thick dust rose like a cloud, so that people could barely see each other. She had barely finished this word when behold! soon a pleasant rain began to fall, not heavy, but [a gentle] spray so that it stopped the dust.

She gained confidence through the Savior's great condescension and said, "Lord, as a proof of Your favor, allow me to be part of the Lord Bishop's holy rites today quietly and without the pressure of other participants." And this happened. The crowd of people was so great that many were crushed and died. She however, although she was weak, arrived at the choir without harassment, where the Lord Bishop consecrated the chrism in her presence. And with great physical comfort and much greater spiritual consolation, she listened to the service, and the Lord Bishop gave her the Body of the Lord with his own hand.

Chapter 76. Regarding this Virgin's Request, how She Asked that the Flow of Tears would be Given Her at Every Seventh Hour of the Day, and that She would be Able to Suffer Much

She also added in her prayer, "Oh Lord, if You would deign to receive my prayers as You have promised me through Your word, give me also this as a sign that tomorrow, that is the day of Your Passion and Death, I will be able to physically suffer and to endure much without failing, and that at all hours of the day, that is the seven canonical hours, You will give me the flow and grace of tears." This was completely fulfilled in her. For the following two nights she spent as if sleepless, sitting up with difficulty, swaying a little. And on the day of the Lord's Passion, she received a thousand blows by flagellating herself with a juniper branch. She covered herself thoroughly in blood, because that branch was so rough, and she did not beat herself lightly. She also said that she endured sweetly [i.e. in good spirits]. And [while] fasting during Easter, she barely ate as much as two morsels of bread, and nonetheless did not grow tired, as she had desired. Also, at Matins and when she read the other hours, such an abundance of tears was given to her by the Lord that at times, she completed the hours only with difficulty because of her tears.

Thus gaining confidence, she prayed and received the answer that her prayer was received favorably. And six persons were pointed out to her by name, and she was told to pray for them. And she was told that for others, she should not begin to pray, because some fell so far from the Lord that they cannot rise up again. Therefore, the Lord said to Jeremiah, "Do not pray for anything good for these people."[37]

Chapter 77. Regarding the Threefold Condition of those in whom the Lord Resurrected Spiritually

On the Day of the Resurrection, when she had taken communion, not having consumed food nor drink until Vespers, she remained, without moving, in one place in the Church, dedicated to her devotion. And there, the hand of the Lord came over her; she saw a multitude of human beings in the light, and the threefold condition of those in whom the Lord resurrected spiritually.

---

[37] See especially Jeremiah 14:12, but also 7:16; 11:14.

In the first group, the Lord stood upright. In this way, good works and their merits seemed to be shaped in them into an image, and God poured Himself into those images, and He brought to life those images by filling them with divine light, and they stood upright.[38] And those were so completely filled with light that they also lit up others. And she was told, "These are those, who keep themselves strenuously in God's service without sparing themselves. They exert themselves intensely beyond what is asked of them, and so much reward is given to them for this that they edify others through the example of a good life. So much is given them through this that they progress within themselves [as well]."

Others were also luminescent, but not as much as those mentioned before, and the image was formed in them similarly through their good merits, in which the Lord poured Himself by illuminating it. And in this, the Lord sat with the image. And it was said to her that those were the ones who do the good, to which they are held, however, [they do it] with physical comfort, and they do not tire themselves much with physical [devotional] practice.

Others were not luminescent, except in so far as the image extended to them, which was formed and illuminated as among the first and second, and in this one, the Lord lay down with the image. And she was told, "Those are certainly good human beings, yet they are remiss, proposing to themselves to do much good, but negligent in the execution."

Chapter 78. Regarding the Blood-letting of this Maiden

Once, when she underwent bloodletting, the blood almost boiled [foamed] because of the heat so that the barber-surgeon and as well as she wondered about it, because her food was meager and simple, she did not use any stimulants [spicy herbs] and fasted every day. Still, the blood boiled hot. And as she was puzzled, she heard a voice within herself saying, "This heat does not stem from nature, but from grace, because God ignites the soul with divine heat, and warms the soul kindled in such fashion. And this is the reason for this heat of the blood." As stated above, during divine visitations, her chest was

---

38   See chapter 69, which suggests that the act of understanding God's will allows for human transformation as *imago Dei*; in this case, the agent is ethical conduct. The remarkably thoughtful theological underpinnings of Agnes Blannbekin's visions deserve thorough study, especially in terms of incarnational motifs which include not only human nature, but all of creation.

often was filled with heat, so that the heat diffused throughout her body burning her sweetly, not painfully.

When the voice spoke to her, she felt stupefied, not out of fear, but with a certain joy, since, as she said, whenever that voice spoke to her, a sudden and unexpected joy jolted her into a stupor at the beginning of the speech. This resulted in a little loss of consciousness; and the weakness that grabbed her was like that which somebody felt when news is announced about a friend whom he loves very much: "Your particular friend is here."

When she regained normal consciousness, she thought to herself whether she could possibly become ill from such an inflammation of the blood as described before, if she would not bleed. The voice immediately replied that this could happen, because the excess of heat in the blood itself could become so great that nature could not bear it. Bloodletting therefore leads to a diminishing of the heat, which makes it more tolerable. And the voice added by saying, "Sometimes, blood will distribute that heat throughout the whole body to all limbs so that, when the blood has become hot through devotion, all limbs become pleasantly warmed, but without sexual overtones and blemish."

Chapter 79. Regarding the Horror of this Virgin's Sadness

One day, after she had taken communion, she was filled with the usual sweetness of that life-giving manna in her bodily as much as in her spiritual sense of taste. And after she remained in this state for a certain part of the day, she began to lose her physical strength. And because the time arrived to say the canonical hours, she tore herself away from that consolation and discharged of her duty to God by reading the hours. And because of this she fell into great sadness, thinking about her miseries and defects, which she began to exaggerate and to magnify, although in truth she was not poor but rich in grace.

And after a short time, she was granted a state of ecstasy, and a voice spoke within her, reprimanding her for her sadness. And it was shown to her that as she cleaned her teeth with a knife that she owned, she pulled two flies from her teeth. And soon thereafter, when she returned to a normal state of consciousness, she heard the usual voice saying to her rather harshly, "As these flies are disgusting to humans, so is your sadness to God."

Chapter 80. Regarding the Fortification of Priests and Other Persons during Partaking of the Body of Christ

Since she felt that during the partaking of the Sacred Body of the Lord, she was physically weakened because of the strength of the Spirit, she thought about how it was for the priests, who participated in communion every day, and why they did not weaken. And she was answered, "Since good and devout priests receive nourishment from the universal Church, and because they consume the Body of the Lord for all the faithful, therefore the devotion and the merit of the faithful provide them with strength." And the following comparison was given to her: "When someone weak is led to good air, where there is sweet scent, although he would have eaten nothing, his brain and heart would be invigorated through the good smell and the good disposition of the air. Likewise, they have another nourishment, that is, when God fills the soul of devout priests with the heat of devotion, the soul infuses heat into the blood and makes it warm, and from this the body receives strength to endure much, such as fasting, abstinence, vigils, the suffering of cold and hardship. The devout person is able to suffer more than other human beings, because he is also strengthened physically by the spirit.

"Likewise, because the male heart is by nature stronger than that of women, therefore devout women weaken more easily in the intensity of devotion than men."

She also thought then of a certain friend of hers, of how he was faring. And it was said to her, "Since he is also infused with the warmth of devotion, he is therefore physically strengthened, so that he can easily suffer much, vigils and other physical hardship. He also sucks sweetness of devotion and strength from the consideration of the devotions of devout persons and the exploration of truth and devotion just as if someone sucked the sweet juice from a grape or another sweet fruit."

In regard to what she said about the soul's divinely infused heat also warming the blood and invigorating the body, she added this: when it is not too strong. Because if there is an excess of heat, the body's powers will be weakened.

Chapters 81 and 82. Regarding the Reprimand of this Virgin, who did not Want to Hear the Voice within Her, Wanting to Dedicate Herself to Other Matters, and Regarding the Sadness which Filled the Heart of this Virgin from Easter to Pentecost

Another time, when she had taken communion on the fourth Sunday after Easter, the voice, which used to speak within her, spoke again. She truly refused to pay attention to the talking voice, intent on dedicating herself to other matters, and tried with great effort to avert her mind from it. And when she had struggled for so long and did not prevail, the voice said to her, coaxing her amicably: "Why are you hostile towards me? I did nothing to you. And although you have seen much in the wide expanse of the mind, you are nonetheless ignorant of what God intends with you." She truly did not now either turn toward the voice that consoled her, because from the time of Easter to Pentecost, sadness had filled her heart. And even though the Lord visited her frequently with divine visitations and in the blessings of sweetness, her heart could nonetheless not free itself from sadness.

Then the voice spoke to her again: "Your heart is adjusted to the [ecclesiastical] season. The time of Advent and the Nativity were filled with joy, when the sayings of the prophets were recited, such as 'Drop down, ye Heaven, from above, and let the clouds pour down righteousness'[39] and similar sayings. Likewise, the time of the Nativity was full of joy. And other times were happy for the apostles, when the Lord was with them in body. Yet because at this time, the apostles and disciples of the Lord did not have the presence of the Lord [among them], and were not yet filled with the Spirit of the Paraclete, they were not able to be consoled sufficiently, however much the Church may celebrate the joy of resurrection."

Chapter 83. Regarding this Virgin's Consolation and Affliction

She did not acquiesce to this so that she could be consoled, but thought doubtfully, "Perhaps this is not the cause of the sadness." Then the voice spoke to her again, "You do not know", it said, "what may be the cause of the sadness for you. A soul affected by divine desire simply does not accept consolation as long as she does not receive what she desires." Through these words, her heart yielded, affirming through further reflection that this was true. And soon, her soul began to languish in intense desire and to thirst for God. And in

---

[39] See Isaiah 45:8.

this listlessness of desire, she made me understand that her soul was consoled as well as afflicted. Therefore, she said, "Although I may be so greatly afflicted within my soul that all my limbs appear to me externally to be languishing in exterior [i.e. physical] torpor, I want nonetheless that this weakness may never cease, but gradually increase until death."

A little while later, when she was by herself, she began to wonder whether due to this sadness, which results from the delay of the desired God and the affliction caused by the languor of the desire for God, God might distance Himself from the soul in such a state, and would be less accepting of a soul in this state than He would be of a soul stimulated by an abundance of joy and consolation by the Spirit. When she considered this, a voice within her answered, "A soul over-flowing in spiritual consolations and the delights of inner joys is given this by God, as much as she is capable of receiving it, and this assures her of future joys given to her by God. Yet a soul affected by yearning for divine love and languishing after God with all her inward being is in this most pleasing to God: thus changing, she assesses Him [His presence] carefully and also responds to God because of the good things that she has received from Him."

Chapter 84. How She was Accusing Herself of the Fear that She had Prayed too Arrogantly, and Regarding [God's] Delight in the Prayers of the Just

One day, when she prayed before the ciborium, where the Body of the Lord was placed, she remembered a certain friend of hers, who frequently asked her to pray for him. While praying, she thus said, "Oh Lord, if there is anything about me that you should take any kind of delight in, I pray to You that you embrace my friend with the same delight as myself, so that he shall please You in the same way." When she had asked for this, however, her heart soon became sad, because she feared that she had prayed too arrogantly and presumptuously. And she was accusing herself, because she might have considered something about her pleasing to God and put herself above her friend in her prayer. Nonetheless, she had not prayed because she thought herself to be put above him, but because she desired the same good-ness for her friend as for herself.

Then God's voice said to her, "God wills that He will be prayed to by sinners also, and this pleases God, because a sinner realizes that he can have nothing except from God. The prayers of the just give God much more joy and delight. God is delighted and cheerful similar to any great prince, in front of whom actors and entertainers present their art and their various games. Thus God is pleased and joyous about various devotions and the devoted prayers of the just. Therefore pray safely, because God is willing to give more to human beings than a person is willing to pray for."

Chapter 85. Regarding the Lord Carrying an Axe on His Left Shoulder

One evening, when she was at home in her praying cell, the Lord appeared to her, after the hand of the Lord came upon her. He appeared in white linen clothes resembling a priestly stole and aprons, His face serene and beautiful, but serious. The diadem on His head was made of nothing but light. On the left shoulder, He also carried an axe. And stepping forward, He said, "I am going to cut down a large tree, which is on earth." Then the virgin feared that it was by chance Pope Nicholas IV,[40] and she wished in her heart: "Oh, if it is the Pope, He will make me very fearful! But if it might be a great king without faith, He will fill me with sweetness of spirit." And soon, she felt both fear as well as spiritual consolation.

Then the devout person said to the Lord: "Oh Lord, what do you want to do?" And the Lord said to her: "You are remarkable! You do not let me cut down and take revenge! Therefore, human beings do not care about me, nor do they fear or venerate me." Then she thought in her heart, "You just said however, oh Lord, that You wished to save a human being." As she thought this, the Lord said, "You are all holding Me back." And the Lord took the axe from His shoulder and brandished it in His hand. She understood through that motion that many would be felled by death, especially great men.

And the Lord pointed the sharp end of the axe forward and said, "When I begin to cut down, I will cut a big wound."

Chapter 86. Regarding the Repeated Apparition of the Lord, Holding an Unsheathed Sword in His Hand, not Raised, but Lowered.

On the following day in the morning, when she came to the church of the friars before Prime, the hand of the Lord came upon her. She saw the Lord in white clothing as on the day before, His face serious and handsome, holding in His hand an unsheathed sword, not raised, but

---

40 Nicholas IV worked toward controlling and standardizing the order of Franciscan tertiaries. He died on April 4, 1292.

lowered. And He said, "I want to cut with my sword, terrify human beings on earth, and instill fear in them!" When she saw and heard this, she became sad and prayed to the Lord that He would remove those terrible visions from her, because she was not the right person to mitigate His wrath, but rather to increase it. She thought bitterly and sadly whether He wanted perhaps to destroy the whole region. And she heard the voice say, "I will not go that far." And she wondered about the fact that the voice, which usually spoke within her, now spoke about itself in the first person, saying, "I will do this", or "I will not do this." Earlier, the voice spoke always in the third person, as it is in the revelations above and in the second to last revelation [chapter 84], where the voice does not speak as if of itself: "God wants that He is prayed to with requests."

Then the voice said to her, "An angel does not have a place in the soul, but only God, who once spoke through Blessed Gregory, when he wrote and interpreted Sacred Scripture: 'It is Me Who speaks within You.' "[41]

She then thought, however, whether all would become true that was revealed to her about these horrifying intentions. And the voice said to her, "All is true, but not all will come about, because good and devout human beings avert God's wrath. And because of this, God in His compassion prepares these revelations for you, desiring to be asked to calm His wrath."

Chapter 87. Regarding a Certain Book by Bernard about the Song of Songs, which her Confessor Wanted to have Copied for the Convent

Soon afterwards, however, this vision came to her: namely, she saw the Lord in white clothing as before and a foundation as if for a building. At that hour, however, when she was in this vision, the friar, her confessor, conducted Mass. And it was shown to her that the said friar had a book by Blessed Bernard about the Song of Songs, which this friar wanted copied for the convent. And the Lord said to the friar, "Take the book and divide it into five parts, and place them into the foundation instead of five foundation stones." The friar did this. And it was given her to understand that the foundation itself is God.

The first part of the book replacing part of the foundation signifies

---

41 Perhaps again a reference to Gregory of Nyssa (d. 395); Gregory's most famous exegetical writings are *In canticum canticorum homiliae* (*Sermons on the Song of Songs*) and *De vita Moysis* (*Concerning the Life of Moses*). See also chapter 38, n. 24.

the friar who out of devotion intended the book to be copied for the use of the friars. The second part signifies the resulting book's future usefulness for human beings. The third part signifies Divine love, which ought to be incited in devout hearts through the script and the use of the book. The fourth part signifies the resulting future praise of God, not only here, but also in the fatherland. The fifth part signifies the sweetness of Divine consolation generated in the hearts of the devout.

And she was told that not only the letters of this book, but all of sacred scripture is placed into this foundation for the construction of a spiritual edifice. And she was told that the Lord is incomparably more grateful for a spiritual edifice of this kind in devout souls than for a church building made of whatever material.

Chapter 88. Regarding Verbal Amusements and Laughter and Other Things of this Type among the Religious

After this she came to herself, and when the above mentioned friar left the altar, another friar approached, intending to read Mass. And when she came into the spirit again during Mass, it was shown her that the friar who read Mass had crowns of white roses, which that friar broke and scattered. She wondered what that was all about. And she was told, "The white roses signify the holiness of the friar's life. But that he scatters the roses signifies verbal amusements, which cause laughter and giggles, which in the presence of God are very noxious to His sanctity." And the Divine Voice added, "It is very reprehensible, and this kind of frivolity among the religious displeases God, because, no matter how jokingly, many lies are spread through this."

Chapter 89. Regarding Two Nets that Span the Whole World, and their Interpretations

One day, when this virgin had taken communion, and the Lord had comforted her with a taste of spiritual and also physical sweetness from the Lord's Body, the Hand of the Lord came over her, and she saw two nets that covered the whole world. One was completely black and enclosed beneath it were all sinners entangled through venial and mortal crimes. And many tried to pass through the net, like a caged bird that struggles to escape the cage, but is not able to. Some in this net lay on their backs without moving. They signify desperate human beings who do not have the will to improve their life, but intend to end it in sin.

The second net, however, had five distinct colors. In some places it was red, in others it was blue-gray, in others black, and in others yellow, in others white. This net enclosed nobody, but it had human beings walking on it, so that there was nobody who was not entangled in the net. Now entangling the feet and falling, they soon broke hands and feet; now the head of some who were falling was separated from the torso, but in such a way that life remained in both, that is in the amputated torso and head. Others gravely stumbled when walking. She saw many falling in this way who were dear to her in the Lord; and she became sad and did not yet understand the vision.

Then the Divine Voice, which usually spoke to her, explained to her the first net, as has been described above. It said that the second net stands for the obstacles of the present life, so that there is not one human being who does not sin. Those who walk on the net's red area are persons afflicted by physical labor, exhaustion, and mental worries over alimentary necessities and who provide for themselves and their families. Yet they fall and break their legs, because they themselves impede their own good will and good intentions that lead to [good] works. Breaking their hands during the fall signifies that they are satisfied with the mediocrity of their good works. And because they have to labor for the necessities of life, it seems enough to them, whatever little devotional exercises they engage in.

The blue-gray area signifies frivolity of mind, however without mortal sin. And those who are walking in this area fall like the first group. Those moving in the yellow area are good prelates: the color yellow is a heavenly color and signifies right intention, which they possess when they correct [others]. Falling the most frequently, they are decapitated, because they offend through the extraordinary harshness of ruling over and superintending their subordinates. However, because righteous intention and zeal for justice motivate them, head and trunk remain alive, and they do not sin mortally, though they offend gravely and frequently in this way. They also seem to tighten the holes and snares so that they do not fall deeply into the net and walk more easily across it. That is, they are excused through [their] correct intention and are spurred on through a zeal for justice, so that they are held accountable for less.

Those who are walking in the black area of the net are those vexed by carnal temptations, avarice, and the like. Those who are walking in the white part of the net are spiritual persons, who strive for a holy life as much as they can. And these got entangled less and moved more easily, yet nonetheless, they also got entangled.

The devout priests tripped less than other good persons because of the support of the Sacred Eucharist, which they consumed regularly and with devotion, yet they got ensnared also. For no mortal, no matter how just, can cross the net without obstacle and without venial sin.

Chapters 90 and 91. Regarding a Certain Priest Celebrating a Second Mass, and her Own Self-Reproach, that is that of the Virgin, and about her Desire and the Instruction Regarding her Prayer and her Thinking.

One day, when she listened to Mass, she was taken aback by the priest without knowing the reason. Then the Divine Voice said to her, "Today, this priest is reading a second Mass without having received sacramental grace before or receiving it now." And then the hour approached when the priest would consume the Lord's Body, and the virgin received a physical taste of miraculous sweetness as if she had received the Lord's Body sacramentally. Nonetheless, she felt an indescribable spiritual sweetness in her soul.

After Mass, she therefore inquired who that priest might be. And she was told by someone from that church that he was a priest who on that day had also read a Mass elsewhere, and that this Mass was his second, which he celebrated in order to make a living. Then she felt pity because of that priest's indigence. And finally returning to her heart [i.e. her feeling, thinking self], she began to reproach herself and spoke in her heart, "Oh you poor little thing, would you only be able to think about yourself alone and concern yourself with how you could reach out to your own desire."

It was her desire, however, that she would always carry the Lord as a loving memory in her breast. As she was thinking about this, the Divine Voice said to her, "You can obtain what you desire, if you will do as I tell you. When you begin to eat food, [but] before you put nourishment into your mouth, pray in your heart to God as follows: 'O Lord, I pray to You that as the superior substance of this dish physically moves into my body and blood, and its inferior nutritional substances go into the lavatory, so should Your best gifts pass into the spiritual nourishment of my soul. Whatever is not beneficial for my soul, should be repelled from her.' When you are working, en route for an indulgence and similar matters, think of the Savior's work, how He has labored for you. Include Him in your works, how He Himself included all in his works, who were prepared to do His will, carried as if in the arms of love, in the way a mother carries a child in

[her] arms. You are recompensing God for the labor and the exhaustion that He endured for you.

"When you are in prayer, desire first for yourself the sweetness and fire of devotion, and through that you will make known to all saints that you are God's daughter, and they will achieve an increase of grace for you. Since if they see the renewal of the heavenly city and the regeneration of their bodies accelerated [through your devotion], they all will feel great happiness. Then expand [your focus] outwards to your fellow human beings, desiring all the while in your heart that if you were able to, you dearly wished to soften God's wrath, which all sinners deserve. And in this you respond to the Divine honor of the Son of God, who came to reconcile sinners to God the Father. Likewise desire in your heart God's grace for all which will be saved. Never is desire from a heart engaged like this disappointed, because everybody receives grace at all times when God is generous."

Chapter 92. Regarding a Certain Friar who, Preaching about St. Francis, Commended him much too Boastfully[42]

At one point, a certain friar preached about Blessed Francis and commended him much too boastfully, preferring him to Blessed Peter and other apostles and saints, so that the audience was scandalized. And this virgin was also present, but was very pained because of this. Then the inner voice said to her, "Look, God will allow the greatest ignominious affliction to happen to this order because of such arrogance and bragging, since such exaggeration and devaluation of the saints displeases Him." One of the prelates, however, namely the custodian, was present at the sermon when that friar preached, and he and other friars were very disturbed by this one friar because of his sermon. Therefore, the custodian called together the older friars, reprimanded him sufficiently, and caused him enough embarrassment and punished him, when he had admitted his guilt. And this happened on the same day, a short while after his sermon.

When it had become late, with the virgin still remaining in the church, the voice came to her [again]. "The wrath of God is calmed, and the Lord is appeased regarding this evil that He said He would bring to the order because of the preacher's excess." Then she thought impatiently in her heart, "How unstable You are, oh Lord!"

---

[42] See note 11. In regard to a scriptural reference about boasting in this context, see 1 Corinthians 31.

In the morning, after she had taken communion, the voice spoke in her again. "Why do you become angry over God's goodness and kindness? He will be conciliatory toward you, as for others, if you yet acknowledge your guilt after the offense. For when God is offended, if a sinner humbly acknowledges the sin, God immediately forgives as it happened to David. He humbly acknowledged his guilt when the angel struck the people. Soon the angel ceased to strike, because God refrained [from punishment].[43] And if a sinner does not admit to his crime and guilt, and nonetheless others pacify the Lord, the Lord will be appeased, as has happened to Job's sons and his friends, for whom Job offered satisfaction by offering a sacrifice."[44]

She, however, did not know that justice was done about the friar's excess, as already stated, so that the Lord changed His decision so quickly. And I remembered the prophet Jonas and the Lord's sentencing of Niniveh, which the Lord retracted so suddenly, even though Jonas was angry.[45] However, I told her how the custodian brought justice to bear on the friar. And then she was comforted by God's goodness.

Chapter 93. Regarding an Offense against the Lord through the Order of the Lesser Brothers, because the Friars Seek God so Negligently

And after the Lord told her this, as it had happened, that the Lord retracts and forgives soon when someone admits his guilt, He added, "With the forgiveness of guilt, the Lord is prepared to add a gift of grace, if there is someone who searches for it." The Lord added also, "The Lord is greatly offended and irreverence is shown to Him in this, that although this order was founded in such holiness and perfection, the friars seek the Lord and Divine grace so negligently."

Then she proposed a defense of the friars, thinking in her heart that because they were engaged in perpetual praise of God, how could they therefore not be seeking God's grace? And the voice answered her that this word was intended not for all friars, but only for those who were remiss, who are the guardians of the norms of the order and believe that they are serving [the order], yet nonetheless make time for jokes and trifles and neglect the grace which the Lord is prepared to offer them, if they seek it with devotion.

---

[43] See 2 Samuel 24:17.
[44] See Job 1:5.
[45] See Jonah 4:11.

She was then shown a young friar of unknown age, who was careful enough in worship, singing and praising God, but lukewarm and remiss in his private devotions. And the Divine voice said, "Friar Nicolas praises God with sufficient liveliness when singing, but because he is negligent in praying to God, he will fall into many tribulations and will be suffering almost unto death, but the Lord will save him from being completely destroyed."

*   *   *46

Chapter 95. Regarding the Timely Choice of Holy Days for Communion, and Regarding the Soul of Every Devout Human Being, that It Is a Sacristy of the Lord and a Pyxis Pleasing to God

Once, when she stood in the church, she was concerned about taking communion of the Body of Christ. For she feared that she would not be able to take communion in a quiet spirit on the day of Pentecost, which was then imminent, because she was to go to another place for some reason, where she feared that the crowd of family members and acquaintances would be too unsettling for her. Therefore she thought that it would perhaps be better to take communion at the Pentecost Vigil, but she desired that this would rather happen on the day of the Outpouring of the Holy Spirit.

When she was so preoccupied with thinking about her concerns, the interior voice spoke to her: "Your mind is limited." And she said that it could be expedient in some cases to move up Holy Days [in order to schedule] communion. "God is not something one can eat, but He is always present in a devout and God-loving soul. And the body of someone who takes communion with devotion is God's sacristy, and the devout soul is a pyxis much pleasing to God, into which God withdraws." And the Divine Voice added that a devoutly officiating priest is a pleasure garden to the Lord, where the Lord loves to rest.

46 Chapter 94 describes six types of supplicant.

Chapter 96. Regarding the Lord's Ascension to Heaven

On Ascension Day, she took communion of the Lord's Body and before communion, she began to think how the Savior's physical departure was so very saddening. And she was used to being often in the grip of sadness during the time when she considered this departure. After she had taken communion, however, the hand of the Lord came over her, and she saw the Lord's ascension in spirit, and remained in this visionary experience almost the whole day until Vespers, yet with one interruption, because once she had returned to herself, not completely, but as if thunderstruck.

Yet when she told me something of her vision, having returned to church about three days later, she began to shiver during Mass because of fear, since she had perhaps talked to me badly and not truthfully. Then the Lord's hand came over her; the Lord deigned to visit her with a new type of vision. After she had knelt and began to ask for replenishments of the spirit before the vision, she got up and opened her eyes, and although the church was filled with people, she saw no one despite her eyes being opened wide. And it seemed to her that her eyes and vision were so dilated that she had eyes a hundred times wider and more open than usual, and she saw [everything] as if in an instant, and she was shown immense and incomprehensible mysteries. And she heard a voice within her say to her, "Look, all this is what was shown to you earlier."

The Lord, however, appeared to her in lovely and attractive human form, clothed with a reddish light as if with a garment, and around Him [was] a small group of disciples, and a countless multitude of angels.

And she heard the Lord say to the disciples, "I am ascending to My Father and your Father, and I take all those with Me, who desire Me in My flesh, having their desire with Me now. I carry My flesh to heaven to My adornment and My pleasure and as a reward, so that it will be rewarded for all that it has endured, and all elect will be rewarded in this, but in different ways. The Martyrs, and those who have suffered for Me, will delight differently seeing it [My flesh]; in another way, the virgins; in another way, the others who are elect."

And the Lord said in addition to the disciples, "If I do not leave, I will not send the Holy Spirit, but if I go, I am sending the Holy Spirit to you, that He will remain with you in eternity."[47]

---

47 See John 20:21–23.

Chapter 97. Regarding the Holy Spirit, Whom Diverse People Receive in Diverse Ways

And it was said to her that diverse people receive in diverse ways. The penitents and sinners abandoning sin receive. Likewise, those receive Him who resolve and strive to progress in what is good, and therefore receive more fully. Also those receive who love God. Also those who are pleased by God in all His works. Those who conform their will to God's will also receive the Holy Spirit superabundantly, so that others are kindled and enlightened by them. In this way the Holy Spirit is given to the disciples, with Whom they subjugate the whole world.

Chapter 98. Regarding the Devil's Deception, how He Deceives Souls

And the interior voice told her that sometimes, Divine fire sweetly ignites the soul inside and all bodily limbs outside. And then the devil strives the most to plant weeds over it, because he has the power given [to him] by God to deceive a human being once in a while in this fashion, like the Blessed Job, so that a human being may be humble and not become insolent through such grace.

It happens that when someone who is not fearful and cautious burns so sweetly in all limbs, the devil offers him sometimes a false sweetness, and therefore, someone [who may be] careless [only] once is brought to ruin. "And this is being tried the most by that good-for-nothing spirit, who appeared to you surrounded by light, and, when you caught him, said to you that he is called 'false light' or 'deceiving light'. He tries to pour the poison of his treachery into those consolations."[48]

After a short while, she began to think as if confounded, that when eager for the sweetness of consolation, a human being would not then be composed [enough] to protect himself, [because consolation] fills the soul through the fire of devotion. Then the voice within her taught her in very polite and well-mannered words and thoughtful paraphrasing how to guard oneself against this. It said, "Yes, one can protect oneself: but one must shield oneself from all contact, which, if one does not pay attention, carries one away." She understood, and [so] enough was being said. The voice also instructed her regarding

---

[48] The name Lucifer literally means "carrier of light". The devil as a being of light is also described by Bernard of Clairvaux, Berthold of Regensburg, and David of Augsburg. See Schmidt, op. cit., p. 361.

menstruating women, that they should shield themselves from too much contact.[49]

Chapter 99. Regarding Three Types of Angels

As was already partially told, the Lord appeared to her as if prepared for ascension, with [her] eyes open but in changed light, and also a countless multitude of angels. She also saw a beam of immense brightness descending from heaven like a wide road, on which angels descended in inexplicable density, nonetheless distinct and without crowding because of their subtle nature. And she said that there were three types of angels. The biggest surrounded the Lord when He was still on earth, and moved closer and closer to Him during ascension. They were completely aglow in the Lord, and conformed to Him in their dress. The Lord, as was said, was clothed in reddish or red light, and so they were fully clothed in red light, so that the six wings and the whole body were red. This red garment was not of just any material, but of purest light, and ended above the Lord's ankles well to the span of one hand, and on the arms it ended also about the span of one hand above the hands. The same is true for the angels. The Lord's hair was long and shiny.

The angels of the second type were clothed in white light, but the wings were multicolored, of miraculous brightness and shimmering beautifully. The third type of angels was clothed as if in golden light. Their wings shimmered with many beautiful colors. She understood indeed that they were the angels who were sent in the service of our salvation. The many colors of the wings signify the variety of virtues that they accomplish in us. And all angels were completely translucent.

Chapter 100. Regarding the Lord's Ascension Proper

While the Lord was still standing among the disciples and the larger angels who shone with a fiery light all around Him, she heard the voices of the angels singing up on high, but she did not see them. After all the angels, even those who surrounded the Lord on earth, descended into the [sphere of the] air, she heard all singing together at the same time. And it seemed to her that they intoned the whole psalm "All people, clap your hands in joy", and some verses of the

---

[49] Agnes's near contemporary, the Beguine Mechthild of Magdeburg (ca. 1212–82), describes menstruation as that "cursed blood" given to all women after the Fall. Schmidt, op. cit., V:9.

psalm "God arises and may His enemies be scattered."[50] They sang, however, in such a way that one choir responded to the other in turn. She also saw an infinite multitude of souls with the Lord. And she said she believed that there were more blessed souls ascending with the Lord than there were Christians alive on earth. And they all together sang with the angels.

And when the angels as well as the blessed souls sang, the Lord ascended with hands placed together in a gesture of devotion, raised up high before His chest, and a little cloud under His feet. And all the blessed ascended with the Lord, with their hands folded in the same way. Yet when the Lord ascended, some angelic choirs preceded Him, some followed, some to the right, some to the left of Him, and they accompanied Him together with the blessed souls. Yet none of the angels touched Him. While all truly rejoiced together in song, the Lord remained silent as long as He ascended through the lower [sphere of] air, and then for the first time began to sing with the others. She also understood that the Lord did this because He never wished to have fun or show signs of exterior gaiety as long as He was in this world.

When she had returned to herself after this great vision, she became very weak in all her limbs and intensely tired in her whole body, but she was strengthened and comforted in her heart.

Chapter 101. Regarding the Lord's First Arrival and the Angels who Are Present at Mass

When she heard Mass during the Octave of the Ascension, she desired to see the Lord, because she had great faith and fervent devotion for Him. Then the voice within her spoke and said, "Look, the Lord said to His disciples during The Ascension that He would return again and that they should see Him. 'Seeing Him' refers to the Day of Judgment, when all human beings will see Him. 'Returning' refers however to the daily arrival, when He arrives in the mystery of the altar, and as many angels assist Him there, wherever that mystery is performed by whatever priest, as accompanied Him during His Ascension."

---

[50] See Psalm 47:1 and Psalm 68:11.

Chapter 102. Regarding the Withdrawal of the Sweetness of Divine Grace

It happened once that this virgin traveled to a certain town for some business, and there she took communion on the day of Pentecost. And because she felt there little of the usual consolation, she became very dejected. The Lord was in the habit of consoling her daily so that during the Masses that she listened to, she felt an indescribable sweet physical and spiritual taste. When the Lord at some point would withdraw that comfort, which however happened rarely, she became extremely despondent. It happened however now, because she was in the turmoil of the market and worldly noise, that the Lord withdrew from her that consolation for about fourteen days, so that she could only very rarely and only in very small doses taste the usual pleasant aroma of Divine sweetness. As she also said, [this occurred] in the way one touches a little honey only with the tip of the tongue, even if there cannot be a comparison between honey and that sweetness.

Due to such withdrawal of comfort, she became in a way weak in body and soul. She also said that her palate almost dried out and that the [sense of] taste of her tongue became so minute that all that she tasted, however delicate, turned insipid for her as [is the case] for a feverish person.

Chapter 103. Regarding a Miraculous Communion of Christ's Body

Then on the fourteenth day was the feast day of Blessed John the Baptist and she thought of taking communion. The reason was that during the night, when she rested, she felt in her sleep a miraculous sweetness of spirit and sudden change to such a degree that she woke from her sleep. And so drunk with the spirit and filled with immense gladness, she jumped up, raised her hand toward heaven, and began to give thanks to God by saying, "Come, oh Holy Spirit!"[51] For she believed that it was the feast day of Pentecost.

With exhilarated spirit, she then went to church and took communion. And soon, when she took the Lord's Body in her mouth, she sensed a physical taste of indescribable sweetness, and felt nothing of the bread's attributes or quality either in taste or touch, nor the rough texture of all the briefly referred to qualities. And this living and true manna, not chewed or in any way touched by her teeth, suddenly descended to her depths with immense sweetness, causing

---

[51] See John 20:22.

change around her in the spirit as well as in the body. And it seemed to her that the heart and all depths became enlarged to make space for her Savior, and everywhere she felt nothing but that sweetness of manna, which nobody can know if he has not received it.

And when she came into ecstasy there, she saw much that she did not know how to communicate, because, I believe, it did not please the Lord that this should be revealed to anybody. She told me at some point that it happens often that something which she has received in a revelation, which seemed to her extremely difficult or even impossible to recount, and already had lapsed from her mind, returned to her memory so quickly and could be told with such ease that she was very astonished. She understood it to be God's will that she would disclose what had been revealed to her to me, a poor and unworthy sinner, and also what was uttered by the Divine voice, who used to speak to her.

Chapter 104. Regarding the Question [Posed to] the Lord, Why He Withdrew Grace

Thus the sweetness described above remained in her well unto noon. Before noon, however, she went to the church of St. Stephen to the ciborium, where Christ's body is housed. There, she showed her reverence and in an intimate manner spoke in her heart, "Lord, for what reason do You do this? Why have You withdrawn from me for so long?" Then the voice said to her, "As a delicate dish tastes good to a famished person, so does God delight in the desire of a thirsty soul who searches for Him." Then she answered, "Yes, Lord, so You search in such a way for what belongs to You to delight You. But what will become of us? It is we, however, who have to carry the heavy weight of the delay." Then the voice said to her, "The Lord withdraws Himself to this hour from His friends for the reason that He will [then] be searched for more fervently. And the devout souls, from whom the Lord retreats, carry away a reward. When the Lord returns through the grace of visitation, He gives that bridal soul to the celestial bridegroom in a spiritual wedding. And all sisters of the soul, that is the virtues of the soul, which were poured into her during baptism, become renewed, so that the soul rejoices according to each individual renewed virtue. This could be compared to a man with ten daughters; if he gave one away in marriage, the other daughters, her sisters, would celebrate with the bride and sister and be merry. So does it happen in the soul, because the Lord celebrates spiritual nuptials with her when He visits her again after some delay."

Chapter 105. Regarding the Soul's Ten Daughters

Another day, when she was in a place suitable for devotion, the issue of the ten daughters entered her mind [again] and she desired to know what they signified. She thought namely that the number was not placed there without purpose. Then very soon the voice that spoke within her said, "Seven daughters are the seven gifts of the Holy Spirit, the other three daughters are the three powers of the soul, in which the soul carries God's image."

Chapter 106. Regarding the Devotion of Prayer

On the day of Saint John the Baptist, after None, when she was in church, she thought that it would be devout to fulfill a vow that she had made. She had namely vowed to say two thousand Ave for a certain person, of which she had already said two hundred. Her body, however, was very weak, because her physical powers left her after an ecstasy, and the visitations or revelations. Then the voice that spoke within her said, "God weighs not the multiplication of prayer but the devotion. For that reason, before God one prayer from one devout person about any kind of matter equals sometimes a large crowd of persons in prayer, such as when processions are taking place and the faithful are carrying relics so that they might get something from the Lord." Then she thought, "Oh God, who are those [devout persons]?" And several were revealed to her by name, whose prayer and devotion are precious before the Lord.

Chapter 107. Regarding the Abjection of a Certain Friar, who for this Reason Left the Order

It happened thus that one good, young, and very devout friar was persuaded by the devil to leave the order one night, not led by the frivolity of the flesh, but deceived by something seemingly good. This friar was very popular and beloved by many. He, however, feared being favored by human beings as perhaps he might not be able to save his soul being held in such esteem, and thought to make himself abject. He [therefore] left [the order]. Led by great remorse, he returned very quickly and asked for forgiveness. Yet a rumor spread among the neighbors of the friars that a friar had left the order and returned.

When this became known to the virgin mentioned before, she began to suffer severely and to feel compassion for the friars and the order because of the scandal, and even for that friar, although she did not know who it was. Then the Divine voice who spoke within her, said, "This is the friar", and named him by name. When she realized that such a holy youth was led astray, she began to cry very hard. And the voice said to her, "He sinned gravely and mortally, because he let himself be defeated so quickly and easily, so that he grabbed and kept money against the purity of his [monastic] rule."

She also prayed to God that He might forgive him, and heard the voice, which was somewhat indignant toward her, say, "It is appropriate that he is still without me, and I will remain foreign to him." She responded, "Lord, until when will You remain angry?" And the Lord answered her, "Not until the end".

After not too many days, the Lord appeared to her in [an aura of] intensely bright light and of large stature, and a sphere of great light surrounded the Lord, and that friar, who has already been mentioned, was next to the Lord in the sphere. And the Lord walked, followed by the friar, who asked Him for forgiveness and seemed tiny next to the Lord. Yet the Lord, while walking, did not seem to notice him. Nonetheless, the friar did not cease to humbly supplicate the Lord and did not recede from the Lord's back. Feeling sorry for the friar, she then said to the Lord, "Ah, kind Lord, have pity and give him Your hand." And as she was pleading, and the friar following the Lord, the Lord extended His hand and, gripping the friar by the hand, lifted him up on high and said, "Know that I will not abandon you again."

Chapter 108. Regarding the Preeminence of St. Peter and St. Paul

On the feast day of the apostles Peter and Paul, when she prayed at the hour of Matins, it crossed the virgin's mind[52] which of the two would be greater and more loved by the Lord. Then the voice who spoke within her said, "The Lord has entrusted and given to Blessed Peter that which He loves most tenderly and above all, that is the Church. Yet He gave and committed to Blessed Paul what was greatest and most beloved in the divinity, that is His name, in order to

---

[52] *venit in mentem hujus virginis.* This chapter is interesting in its emphasis on different cognitive approaches to the twofold question; the Latin terms used here, apart from *venit in mentem*, also include *in corde suo cogitavit* and *cogitavit apud se*. Throughout the book, the scribe notes repeatedly how Blannbekin thinks deeply about matters of faith – a far cry from the emerging stereotypical clerical view that a female preponderance for experiential mysticism precludes rational thought. For a scriptural reference about the question of love between Christ and Saint Peter, see John 21:15. This vision is a fascinating creative elaboration of Christ's famous question posed to Saint Peter.

carry it before the nations and kings. Therefore, discern whom God loves more!"

Then she thought in her heart, "Until now, I [still] do not know, who is loved more by the Lord. And I cannot know this through what has been said to me." She desired therefore to know this, who was loved more. Then the voice said to her again, "Blessed Peter was so to speak the leader of the Lord's army and retinue; Blessed Paul was so to speak the Lord's intimate counselor, close to Him in purity. Therefore, discern whom God had loved more!"

She however thought by herself, who was now loved more by God. And for a third time the voice said to her, "Blessed Peter had keen and quick love and impatient love for God, blessed Paul however had slow and thoughtful love for God. Therefore, discern whom God loves more!"

She, however, thought as before that she could not understand who was loved more through this either and stopped to think and worry about it.

When it was morning, she went to church. And when she heard divine service, suddenly a voice within her spoke. "Blessed Peter is loved more by God and is the greatest in the community of saints, since he is the first and superior through the apostolate, the most devoted through the imitation of the passion. He always carried the desire to suffer for Christ in his bosom, and suffered finally a death and passion similar to the Savior's Passion, that is the cross. Likewise, the Savior named him alone and singled him out by name after the Savior's resurrection. These are the preeminent love's three reasons."

At the same time, the virgin began to tire because of grave pain, so that she was not able to visit a church. Having suffered many illnesses in her weak body throughout her life, she said that this head-ache exceeded all other pain. Yet nonetheless, she endured [this illness] gratefully and joyfully and asked the Lord that He might prolong the pain, desiring to recompense His suffering in however small a way.[53] She told me often that deep within her heart, she desired to suffer for God the most ignoble death.

---

[53] To some degree, Agnes models here a Catholic devotional practice that still lives on today, the mission to be a victim soul. St. Therese of Lisieux is perhaps the most famous twentieth-century victim soul, but there are many others. For the separate notion that the degree of suffering determines the extent of divine rewards, see, e.g., chapter 115, which also raises the legitimate question of divine sadism in the face of human suffering.

Chapter 109. Regarding the Defense and Salvaging Explanation of the Denial of the Lord by Saint Peter and Other Disciples

And after she had remained in bed at her house for a few days, one Sunday morning she forced herself with much effort to go to church. Suffering greatly from her headache, she began to think about Blessed Peter – the feast day of Blessed Peter had occurred only recently. She thought that if Blessed Peter had experienced such pain, he would not have denied the Lord, because a human being afflicted with pain would rather take refuge in the Lord. As she thought this, suddenly the Lord's voice spoke in her, "Don't think like this! During the Savior's Passion, the passage of time,[54] the air, and everything else became so mixed up and confused that because of human weakness [and] too much perplexity, Blessed Peter and the others could not stand firm." And she said that the Savior suffered more in [His] compassion for the disciples' confusion.

Chapters 110, 111, and 112. Regarding the Joy and Benefit that a Human Being can Gain from the Devout Recollection of the Passion of Jesus Christ; Regarding Those who were Excommunicated and the Contemplation of Heaven and of the Passion of Christ

The voice also said, "The Savior felt the greatest love for His Passion. As a sign of this love, as the most outstanding memorial of His passion for human beings, He left behind the sacrament of His body and His blood for the reason that a human being ought to continually recollect the Lord's Passion." Then she thought, "And who could endure that the pain of passion would continuously be alive in one's heart?" Then the voice said, "On the contrary, greatest joy can be derived from a devout recollection of the Savior's Passion. Because of the Passion and Christ's Death, there is the sacrament of the altar, through which a devout soul has manifold joys and benefits.

"First, from looking at that sacrament: when someone with devout faith looks at it, that person will always receive some degree of grace; secondly, because of the partaking of communion, which the faithful receive from the altar sacrament when the priest officiates. This

---

[54] Latin *tempus*. Dinzelbacher translates it to mean "weather", i.e. *tempestas*. Although the fact that the word is placed next to *aer*, "air", makes Dinzelbacher's choice plausible, I lean toward the psychological meaning of *tempus*, acknowledging that people's personal sense of the passage of time was confused due to the trauma of Jesus' death.

always profits the universal church. For they receive strength against the temptations of sins from the power of the health-giving host for nobody can resist the devil and one's own inclination if not supported by the sacrament's grace." And she said that all faithful receive grace during communion, even sinners, in that they are obstructed in committing evil that they are intent upon or to which they are instigated. And she presented the following example: "Much like two fighters in the ring who are sometimes protected by two guards, the ring guards,[55] who carry sticks in their hands with which they block blows by the opponent so that the fighters can rest a little." She also said that none who are excommunicated receive some of the grace, although the other sinners receive [grace], as was said [above].

"Second [sic], because the soul who receives this sacrament obtains there first the strength to resist sin and develops a certain holy pride and indignation against sin and begins to despise it. She even scorns the first thoughts and inklings. Second, she develops a certain dignity and free-spiritedness which delights God and in which He prides Himself. Third, the soul develops celestial love for heaven. Fourth, she attracts beauty and the daily renewal of beauty. Fifth, she develops a double wisdom: first, because God makes Himself more known to her and because she knows more; secondly, because He reveals His secrets to her more than to others." She was told all of this when she was in church and listened to Mass.

The voice also said that a soul contemplating heavenly and divine matters could receive greater sweetness, but contemplating the Passion of Christ, it could receive a greater conflagration of love. And she mentioned the example of Blessed Francis.

Chapter 113. Regarding the Kissing of Christ's Wounds and their Visual Appearance and Meaning

On the same day, when she returned to her home, the voice speaking within her said, "A soul who loves God should always contemplate the Lord and kiss His wounds. For the savior's wounds are of such brightness in the glorified body of Christ that they surpass all of the heavenly court in loveliness and joy.

"First, a devout soul ought to contemplate Christ Crowned with Thorns. This ennobles the soul and makes her worthy of the paternal inheritance in heaven with Christ. Second, she should look closely at

---

55 As elsewhere in the text, the scribe inserts a German term to paraphrase the Latin, in this case *Grizwertil*, i.e. "ring guards".

the wound of the right hand: from this she gains liberation and freedom and the gift of [other] presents. Third, she should look closely at the wound of the left hand; from this she gains a shield and protection against temptation. Fourth, she should look closely at the wound of the right foot; from this she gains steadfastness and strength to suffer. Fifth, she should look at the wound of the left foot; from this she gains delight, that is, joyful pleasure[56] in virtues and what is spiritually good."

Chapter 114. Regarding the Accounts of Holy Virgins about What and How Much They have Suffered because of Christ

During these days, around noon, the hand of the Lord came upon her. And the Lord appeared to her in a garment shining like the sun, accompanied to the left and right by two groups of people dressed in white. And the Lord said to her, "Would you not like to be with them?" She said, "Indeed, o Lord". The Lord encouraged her and said, "Find out from them in what way and how much they suffered because of the Lord." And first Blessed Catherine, then Blessed Lucy, Blessed Christina, Blessed Agnes, Blessed Agatha and the other virgins and martyrs who stood to the right of the Lord told her what and how much they had suffered. And they carried their passions with them as if painted on a wooden board and that painting seemed as if alive or having life.[57] Then she thought, "Lord, I am not worthy to suffer for You in such a way." Then the Lord showed her Blessed Job in the second group [of saints] to His left, all of which were of remarkable beauty. And the Lord said, "Since you cannot reach out to martyrdom because of the absence of a persecution of Christians, suffer nonetheless physical infirmities and illnesses out of your free will, together with Blessed Job, who gladly endured them out of love for me." At that time, she suffered from grave physical pain.

---

56 Again, a German paraphrase is inserted, *gelust*, to illustrate the Latin *delectatio*.

57 This description is a fine illustration of much medieval interpretative labor over diffuse and difficult-to-decode visionary images and light phenomena. Already existing visual codes are superimposed on mystical visual data to align them with collectively held belief systems, or visual stimuli serve as trigger or enhancement of visions. See also chapter 123 for another example of this approach. Art historian Jeffrey Hamburger, among others, has amassed much visual data for Christian women's spirituality in fourteenth-century Germany. See, e.g., Jeffrey Hamburger, "The Visual and the Visionary: The Image in Late-Medieval Monastic Devotions", *Viator* 20 (1989): 161–82.

Chapter 115. Regarding the Perfect Reward, which Consists in Patience

And the Lord added, "Someone cannot persevere until the perfect reward if he does not endure voluntarily and patiently the ailments of all joints of his limbs." Then she thought, "Oh Lord, I believed that the perfection of merits and rewards consisted in love." The Lord responded to her, "Someone cannot suffer this voluntarily and patiently without the strength of love." Then she thought, "O Lord, are You enjoying therefore the sufferings and afflictions of those who are Yours?" The Lord answered her, "In this is love pronounced and proven, when someone suffers voluntarily and freely because of the Lord." Then she thought, "Lord, do You love me?" The Lord said to her, "I love, and never has a mother loved the child of her womb as much as I love you. The proof is that I poured out bloody sweat in agony and on the cross I bled whatever blood had remained; and love led me to do this." Then she thought, "O Lord, this is a general love with which You love all Christians." The Lord said to her, "I love you also with a singular love, and the sign is that I visit and console you within yourself in physical illnesses and infirmities."

Chapter 116. Regarding the Stalwart Service of Human Beings and the Greeting of the Minister of the Friars and his Instruction

Then she thought of a certain friend of hers, "Lord, I know that he loves You; and nonetheless he would love You more if he were healthy, so that he can serve you better." And the Lord said, "Whoever serves Me stalwartly and continuously, in his little ship I am and guide and lead it, and what he cannot do, I will bring to completion."

There appeared also a group of friars, who assembled with excellent manners and waited to be greeted by the Lord.[58] The Lord, however, turned to the minister and said, "Greetings, Father! You are the father

---

58 This visionary incident and the following chapter serve so clearly the concerns of the Franciscan scribe/confessor that it is not clear to what extent this material is actually rooted in Blannbekin's mystical experience. It demonstrates, however, that core visionary materials could be stretched and formed to no small degree to suit the interpretive community's need of divine or divinely inspired responses to their problems.

of my sons whom I committed to your faithfulness. If negligence and laxity of the life of the rule should spread because of your sloth, woe to you!" Then the minister fell to his knees and said, "You know that I employ all the diligence I can muster." Then the Lord said, "Be careful of all arrogance in your correction and criticism; be an example to your subordinates so that you will be more often in the choir than your friars. Wherever you are among the friars, you should at least once a day be publicly in the choir for [the reading of] the hours and prayers, in order to be an example to the friars. Be with them during meals and at other [occasions] as much as you can." And when He said this, He looked closely at all prelates, since there were many present, and said, "How much do I hold against you! Be careful that friars do not leave as apostates because of your harshness and other friars are not separated from the Lord because of your strictness! Note that the Lord who said to Peter, 'Tend to my sheep', also told him, 'I do not say this to you up to seven times, but up to seventy seven [times]!' "[59] Then the minister, who humbly fell to his knees again, said, "Lord, I will gladly watch myself in all these matters."

Chapter 117. Regarding the Friars' Custos, Lector, and Guardian

Then the Lord said to the custos with harsh enough words, "Greetings, o Lord! You ought well to be more humble and consider where I took you from and to where I have lifted you up, and to speak more kindly with the friars and correct [them] more gently and not to have such scornful words for the friars!" Then He spoke to the lector, "Greetings, o Lord! You are too lazy and have become lax in your service because of your illness. How long has it been since you have attended Mass? You show too much concern about your health and you are too wasteful with the alms for the poor!"

Then he greeted the guardian by bending down and rebuking him severely. "Although you are a friend of God, you offend greatly because of derisive and jocular words that provoke distraction and laughter. You act like a washerwoman who washes sheets and bleaches them in the sun and then pushes the sheets into the dirt."

59 See John 21:16, 17, Matthew 18:22.

Chapter 118. Regarding the Devout Soul in the Bridal Chamber of Contemplation and the Female Head of the Household who Accomplishes Five Things in her Home[60]

One day, I read to her something by Blessed Bernard [of Clairvaux] on the Song of Songs, how the Soulbride renounces all other affections and throws herself completely into love. She thought about this intensely in her mind and wondered why she [the Soulbride] did not strive for honor, because this also is known from Blessed Bernard's statements that God, inasmuch as He is Bridegroom, does not demand anything but to be loved. And when she contemplated this in her mind, she heard a voice within her saying to her, "The devout soul in the bridal chamber of contemplation, like a bride, does not strive after anything but love. But in all else she resembles a female innkeeper or the female head of the household in the home and a female housekeeper, because in managing the home, a female head of the household accomplishes five things in the house in fear of her spouse and in his honor.

"First, she is circumspect in the education of sons and daughters in customs and discipline. Thus, internally, a holy soul looks with worry upon herself, and externally she provides for the custody of the senses and coordinates internal motion and external manners.

"Second, the female head of the household rules the family by employing [them] in regard to their work debts. Thus, the devout soul subjects the body to indentured servitude and physical works.

"Third, a female head of the household is greatly accommodating in herself and in her works and activities. Thus, the devout soul is well ordered and moderate in all of her activities, that is in vigils, fasts, prayers, and other deeds.

"Fourth, a female head of the household is concerned about the ways in which she may please the spouse and serve his will. And thus the devout soul strives after how to please God and how to implement His will and takes care not to offend Him.

"Fifth, a female head of the household displays compassion and piety towards all who approach her with a request, satisfying each as

---

60 The Cistercian prioress Beatrijs of Nazareth (d. 1268) also employed the image of a female head of a household to describe spiritual growth. See her tractate *Van seuen manieren van heileger minne*, edited by Leonce Reypens and Joseph van Mierlo (Leuven: Vlaamsche Boekenhalle, 1926). Mechthild of Magdeburg also uses this trope to describe her advanced age and role vis-à-vis God as Father, for which the image of a young and alluring bride would be inappropriate. See Schmidt, op. cit., VII: 3.

she is able to do. Thus, the devout soul is prepared to edify or console her fellow man through the help of prayers, counsel, consolations, exhortations and anything else that she is able to do."

And much was shown in this revelation – in what things someone would abound or in what things someone would be lacking. And it was told to her that the soul, inasmuch as she is in the bridal chamber of contemplation, behaves and conducts herself like a bride and does not know anything but to love and be open to love and therefore to strive intensely like a bride, and so on.

Chapter 119. Regarding the Restraining [Powers] of the Just, who Hold God's Wrath at Bay through their Prayers, and Regarding the Protection of Austrian Land[61]

One day, when she prayed for the peace of the land, the voice became present to her as usual and said to her, "I have protected the land in peace long enough, and was wrathful toward the opposed faction. People do not recognize this, but are ungrateful. Therefore I wish to be wrathful towards them!" Then she tried harder with [her] prayers that the Lord would protect the land from enemies. Then the voice said to her, "You are not pious. Why have you not prayed for those in Hungary, where much evil happened to evil people?" Then she said, "O Lord, I did not know of that evil." And she continued to pray to the Lord that He would defend the land. The Lord said to her, "I was always and am now restrained by the prayers of the just." Then she thought, "O Lord, who are those who hold You in their prayers and appease Your wrath?" The Lord said to her, "The suffering, who endure evil patiently while being afflicted. And those who pray with a devout and clean heart and the devout priests who sacrifice the host at the altar." And the Lord said that there were many such priests, but not so many who had [His] full confidence. Then she thought, "O Lord, will You protect us nonetheless?" The Lord said to her, "More than [all of] you trust me." This indeed has happened. Namely, when the Hungarians soon thereafter invaded Austria and the ruin of the land was feared, and people had fallen into despair, and there was neither human counsel nor help, the enemies withdrew from the land and sent a peace delegation and presented themselves to the satisfaction of the duke of Austria and according to his honor [i.e. rank].

---

61 Frequently, women mystics were called upon or felt a mission to influence the outcome of political strife. For a similar chapter, but with regard to a different military conflict, in Mechthild of Magdeburg's work, see Schmidt, op. cit., VII:28.

Chapter 120. Regarding the Blue Coloration of Christ's Body on the Cross and those in Tribulation, What and How They Ought to Pray, and Regarding the Mass of the Holy Cross

One day, when she was in church, she looked at a crucifix, from which the rays of the sun reflected back and hit her eyes. And when she closed [her] eyes, she heard a voice within her saying to her, "Do not fear anything and look again at the crucifix and don't be terrified." Then she opened [her] eyes and looked at the crucifix, in which the sun was intensely reflected, and the image of the crucified appeared, completely blue, and although she was forewarned not to be afraid, she was nonetheless somewhat terrified. The voice said to her, "This is how the dead Lord was mounted on the cross, with blue skin." And the Lord added, "Consider how much affection Joseph had for the Lord at that moment, Whom he took down from the cross and embraced like this, and with great feeling and devotion wrapped in a shroud and buried!"

And the Lord added, "Those who find themselves in tribulation ought to pray to the Lord with the feeling and love that Joseph had for the Lord, and devoutly venerate the Lord's passion. Then the Lord would be favored toward them, because the Lord's passion contains much and plentiful grace. For the Lord displayed more love and dignity in the passion than He ever showed a person." And the Lord added, "Tell your confessor that he read a Mass of the cross every week for the current tribulation! And ask other devout persons that they ask Him through the Lord's passion that He withdraw His wrath from the people."

Then she thought in her heart, "Oh, Lord, be favorably inclined toward us!" And the Lord said, "I will save you and be well-disposed toward you."

Chapter 121. Regarding the Blessed Virgin's Clothing and the Assumption

On the day of Blessed Mary's Assumption, the hand of the Lord came over her. And she received an apparition of the Blessed Virgin dressed in a very white tunic, so that nothing white in this world could be compared to it, and She wore an equally incomparable red frock coat. She was also wearing a very shiny veil. On the inner lining of the veil were very beautiful faces that shone as if [reflected] through glass. She also had a crown with twelve stars on her head. And she was told that the white tunic signifies virginal chastity, through which the Blessed Virgin was assumed [to heaven]. The red frock coat signifies the Virgin's martyrdom, which she suffered during the passion of her blessed son. The translucent veil that covered her signifies saints in the fatherland, who themselves shimmer in love for God because of the Virgin's love and merits.

The interior surface of the veil signifies the Virgin's love and affection, illuminating her before God's countenance. The exterior surface of the veil signifies the Virgin's affection for the human race, through which she protects us always, and this is much like a shield against the wrath of God.

And since then, when this vision was shown to her, the Lord seemed to be wrathful toward His people. For the king of Hungary and the Komai[62] and other infidels brutally invaded the land of Austria and devastated it. She was told that the Lord wished to show a little wrath toward us and then console us, much like a father beats a son with a little switch, then soon after consoles tenderly. This has fully come to pass. Namely, suddenly what nobody had hoped for happened: peace and friendship were forged between the Lord King of Hungary and the duke of Austria.

Chapter 122. Regarding the Complaints of All Elements about Those Who have Taken Religious Vows

At one time, when she came into the spirit, she watched and listened [supernaturally], and a voice came to her that said, "All elements complain about those who have taken religious vows. The fire, that is the fire of Divine Love, complains that certain religious people [i.e. those who have taken vows] repel that fire of Divine Love from themselves in three ways." And when she had heard this voice, she looked and three symbols of those three types of rejection appeared to her. Indeed, she saw boiling pitch and the extremely vile brood of water frogs and a certain type of vermin called a scorpion. These appeared in the middle of the fire, yet in such a way that a certain darkness existed between them and the fire. This symbolizes the external activities and the worldly business transactions in which certain religious persons get involved at times. It also symbolizes the hope regarding [their] savings to which they resort whenever they

---

[62] *Comani.*

wish, taking their financial support from it, [and] also their care for meat in gluttonous desire.

In the same way, the earth is complaining, because, as it was told her, God gave all honors to the earth in that He took His Body from the earth, [and] in that He soaked the earth with His sacred Blood. Also, because His Body of Earth is consecrated daily, and because bread grows from the earth. The Lord did all of this because of that earth who carries the soul, that is the human body. The nature of the human body is taken from the earth to serve God and to train itself bodily in service to God, and because certain religious people do not engage in this, the earth complains.

And she saw there again three obstacles, namely a heap of manure, liquefied pitch, lead and wax mixed together and a light in a black and darkened lantern. These are greed, lasciviousness, [and] physical laziness that stain the soul. Like pitch, they inflame the soul, like liquid lead, which is very hot, they make the soul malleable and soft toward everything reckless much like wax is malleable. The dark lantern represents a lack of generosity and a difficulty regarding obligations, because they are obstinate and sluggish regarding that for which they are held responsible. It is necessary to prod them like cattle, after which they do not offer anything above and beyond in terms of special devotional exercises or devotions.

The air complains, that is the words [utterances] that communicate [through the use of air and vocal chords]. And again she saw three [aspects or things], namely wind and turbulent clouds, flashing and whistling something sweet through a whistle. These are the words of blasphemy and cursing and horrible words; also leisurely chitchat, witty and teasing speech and words that make people laugh.

The water complains, that is the sanctification that is effected by the Holy Spirit. There she saw three [aspects or things], namely turbulent water, white crystals with black spots, and honey spiked with the sharp tips of bee stings sticking out. These represent the violation of baptismal innocence, imprudence regarding tearful expiation [of sins] and the neglect of the sweetness of devotion due to other cares.

The voice appeared for each element that symbolized the aforementioned vices and explained everything as it had been said. This vision, however, included only persons who took a religious vow, whether living in an order or in the world, [and] who were committed to divine service. In each single element she saw many from various orders and ranks that she recognized.

Chapter 123. Regarding the Condition of Different Groups of Human Beings, that Is the Secular Clergy,[63] those in Religious Orders, the Priests, and Good and Bad Laity

On the second Sunday after the Octave of the Blessed Virgin's Nativity, when she was in church at the beginning of Mass, she came into the spirit. Set alight within with divine fire, she saw a great multitude of images surrounded by immense light that represented the condition and life of human beings, of the secular clergy and those in religious orders, the priests, clerics, and the good and bad laity. In the image of each was expressed much good and bad that belonged to each. And she recounted that this was so familiar and intelligible to her as if she had looked at these regularly.

Some showed themselves with a terrifying appearance, and, as she said, the bad priests looked more horrible than the other sinners did, so that even she became frightened. And if the Lord would not have consoled her a little beforehand and soon after with a pleasant revelation, she would have been too terrified. The bad priests actually were completely naked and very black. They wore a round diadem around the head that signifies priestly dignity and authority. Indeed, all priests wore round diadems, as the saints are painted, but differentiated according to their merits. The diadem of bad priests was black in color and made of pitch and covered their hair. Their faces were black, their eyes torn out, and the teeth horrible. They were smeared with human excrement all over their chests, which signifies the ugliness of their heart's concupiscence. Their hands were dipped in blood and dripped blood. This signifies that they handle the Lord's Body with disrespect, as it was explained to her after the vision by the voice, and it also signifies the injustices and violence that they incur upon their subordinates during excommunication and the withholding of sacraments.

The good priests, however, were clothed with sacred white priestly garments, which signify the purity of body and soul. The stole was made of pure gold, which symbolizes their love. The maniple on the left hand was embroidered with several [colors], which represent the diversity of virtues. Their faces were suffused with red and white color and were translucent. The round diadem on their head was of a certain light, like rosy sunlight, yet although the face was shining and the diadem glowed in a similar fashion, both types of light were clearly distinct from each other. And nobody wore a diadem except the priests alone, because it signified sacerdotal authority as has been

---

[63] *statu secularium.*

said. On their feet, they wore footwear made of flowers, which signifies gentleness, inasmuch as flowers are gentle when touched.

In a similar vein appeared the good deacons and sub-deacons in their adornment, and likewise the distinctions between good and bad married people. The bad looked dirty and vile, but the good truly were made up beautifully, some more so, some less so depending on their merits. And all their merits and misdemeanors were clearly recognizable in their images. And so far, there was not one who was perfect or beautifully adorned in whose face or clothing something ugly could not be found. All virgins were clothed in white garments, which signifies purity, and they wore crowns on their heads without a [fully closed] circumference, which signifies the imperfection of the sanctity in their current life.

Chapter 124. Regarding this Virgin's Special Devotion, who Used to Say Six Our Fathers Every Day, and Regarding Compunction, Faith, Love, Desire for God, Help from the Blessed Mary, and the Passion of Christ

Out of special devotion, this virgin was used to say every day six Our Fathers and as many Hail Marys. One time, however, when she was lying down, six knights appeared and stood around her.

The first knight was clothed in white garments and was called Compunction. He had a red shield, which signifies contrition and affliction of the heart over sins. Stars, signifying the innumerable amount of forgiven sins, also surrounded him. He carried a sword of heavenly color in his hand.

The second knight was [sic] and was called Faith, clothed in gilded garments, carrying a sword in a golden color, which signifies the preciousness of faith. On the sword was a living eagle that symbolizes the sacrament of the Body of Christ. He held a sword of steel in his hand more radiant than the sun that signifies the strength of faith, through which all temptation can be overcome.

The third knight is [sic] and was called Love, and was clothed with the sun. He had a golden sword, which signifies spiritual honor and a religious attitude in words and habits. His shield was made of the light of celestial brightness, and it had a coat of arms which was called eternal life, and it had now the form of a child, then of a youth, now of the crucifix, then of a lamb. And the knight said, "Look, the Lamb of God, look, that will take away the sins of the world."[64]

64　See Revelation 22:1, 2.

The fourth knight was called Desire for God and was dressed in various colors. He held a sword in his hand and a shining shield in the form of a clear torch, which contained an image or a face with a diadem, which signifies that the devout soul always desires God's gaze and face. And this knight was shorter in stature than the others.

The fifth knight was called the Blessed Virgin Mary's Help. He had a shield in which were the mother and child. And the knight said, "In whatever direction I will have lifted the shield, there I am triumphant over enemies!"

The sixth knight was called the Passion of Christ or Christ's Death. His shield was covered with blood and very radiant, with the crucifix contained in it. And the knight said, "Christianity endures because of the strength of this blood, and in no other way could it endure." His sword was the wooden cross; his garment made of switches, which signify the vestiges of the switches of the flagellated Christ.

Chapter 125. Regarding a Demon who Wished to Confuse Her

Yet when these six knights whom I believe to have been angels, stood around her and spoke to the virgin, behold! From across the room in a corner, a demon appeared. He tried to interfere so that the virgin would not be able to focus on those six knights by interjecting comments such as, "O, how big a ruckus and noise these mice make!" He also said, "Look, the door is not secured with a lock, and thieves will enter any minute now." He wished to confuse her with other similar comments, but was unable to. For she was absorbed in a miraculous consolation of the spirit during this vision.

Chapter 126. Regarding a Certain Youth who Joyfully Received Each Single Brother at the Door Entrance and Led Them Inside

Once in the spirit she saw the friars congregating before the refectory at the hour of breakfast, as was the custom. And when they entered at [the sound of] the bell, a certain youth, nicely dressed, stood in the door entrance and joyfully received each one of them and led them inside. And when the friars had seated themselves at the table, that youth passed before everybody and made the sign of the cross. Finally, he came to a Lector and said to him, "O you lightweight fellow,[65] how rarely do you extend a benediction to me!" which was a reprimand, because he rarely ate in the refectory.

[65] *domicelle.*

Chapter 127. Regarding the Extinction of Fire in the House and the Star that Appeared on the Firmament

Once during the night of Advent, on this Sunday, that is the first, she felt special devotion and was used then to take communion of the Body of the Lord; at this hour then she wished to read Matins. However, the fire had gone out in the house, so that she didn't have light, which made her feel very wretched. For she feared that she would not be able to take communion, because she could not read the nightly office. And so she anxiously opened the window of the room and looked onto the ground or street [to see] if perhaps someone from the city guard might walk by who could ask for some fire from some other house in the neighborhood.

And with the window open a star appeared on the firmament toward north next to Ursa Major, from which something like a burning candle was handed down [to her]. It was the length of barely one finger, and gave her fully sufficient light through the room's window. When she had then opened the book, she read Matins – and in a book which had very small letters! And this attests even more to the miracle, that this light did not shine anywhere else except over the letters and the script of the book.

Wondering about this, she wished to try something and put her hand over the book in that light; and then she did not see the hand and they were [both] dark. Likewise, it was dark on the margins of the book, and only where the script was, was there light. And soon after she had finished Matins, that light and illumination disappeared.

Chapter 128. Regarding the Resurrection of the Lord and the Closed Grave

At a time, when she remained in church during the night of Easter at the hour of Matins, she began to think after Matins that it was not incredible that a virgin gave birth to the God man. This, however, was very much to be admired: that the great man would come out of and be resurrected in a closed grave, with a rock rolled before it. The choir of the church in which she was at the time, however, was closed and secured with a bolt inside the door, and a big wooden wedge was firmly driven between the door and the bolt so that the bolt could not be pushed away [from outside the door]. The middle wall, which separated choir and church, was elevated all the way up to the dome of the choir so that nowhere was an opening to even a small passage.

And as she was reflecting on this, as has been said, behold! The wedge was noisily pulled away from the space between door and bolt and, through Divine force, passed through the closed door in the choir and fell before the face of the said virgin in a great fall on the stones of the floor. Although it did not touch her, it caused her sudden great panic. When she had pulled herself together again, she prayed to the Lord and said, "Lord, You have frightened me enough today, console me now!" And soon she fell into a light sleep, and she stretched out over the stones of the floor.

Then the Lord appeared to her,[66] carrying a bowl in His hand, in which were a piece of fried fish and a honeycomb. And the Lord said to her, "Eat!" She said to Him, "Oh, if You were to eat, I would eat much more willingly." Then the Lord broke something like a small piece off the fish and dipped it [in the honey] and put it in His mouth and tasted it. The remaining piece He put in the mouth of the virgin. And the Lord said, "Now it cannot seem to you that something might be difficult for God [to do]? Because, whatever God wishes, that is very easy and feasible." The Lord showed her through this that as that solid object [i.e. the wedge] could move through another solid object [i.e. the door], so the reanimated Body of the Lord moved through and left the closed grave. This virgin told me that from that day on, that is Easter, until the Day of Ascension all that she tasted and ate had the flavor of honey.

Chapter 129. Regarding a Multitude of Human Beings and Angels

In the year of the Lord 1281, brought into the spirit on the feast day of St. Michael, she saw an infinite assembly of human beings and angels descending from heaven. They descended in groups on nine roads sufficiently wide for human beings and worked with them for the success of the nine gifts or virtues.

The first gift was knowledge of self.

The second knowledge of God.

The third the increase or rise of grace.

The fourth praise and honor of the Lord.

---

[66] This is one of the few recorded dream visions and one of several mystical experiences that do not occur in a liturgical context. Given that the *vita* documents only select events from Agnes's life, we may assume that she had many more dream visions and sacred experiences than her scribe was able to record.

[67] See Luke 24:42, 43.

The fifth was the joint usefulness of all faithful, the living as much as the dead.

The sixth was the renewal of grace.

The seventh contempt for things of the earth and the rise or the promotion of desire for what is above.

The eighth the view or manifestation of the divine presence.

The ninth was the exalted consummation or consummated exaltation in divine love.

The first group of angels prepared the Lord's road for a person. In order to signify this, they carried tools in their hands useful for preparing the way, such as spades and so on. Those tools were bright and luminescent and of delicate material. The angels of the second road carried lights that were very bright and flaming. The third [type of] angels carried in their hands something like full pouches. And they carried those small pieces of baggage from the Lord to human beings and back from human beings to the Lord, but what they carried to the Lord seemed to be much more expensive and valuable.

The fourth carried tubas in their hands, and played them. The tubas were actually formed as follows: the length of the tuba was whiter than snow, the knob resembled gold, [and] the mouthpiece of the tuba, which was placed [on the mouth], was red. The fifth carried in small bells something like precious pearls and distributed them among the human beings and brought some of these gifts down to the souls in purgatory. The sixth burned completely, because fire brings renewal, and they worked with each other for the renewal of grace. The seventh shook something seemingly disgusting off their hands while trying to pull upwards. The eighth had divine faces, each one of them as if representing God's face. The ninth were placed like a crown, so that a big group was in each crown. And one crown was arranged above the other up to the heavens to the Divine Countenance. And those did not descend to human beings, but waited for human beings as if to crown them in the next life. The human beings actually moved forward in different ways because of these angelic visitations, since some moved forward in certain gifts [i.e. virtues] mentioned above, others in several, some more, some less.

Chapter 130. Regarding a Certain Castle and her Explanation

Having come into the spirit again after a few days, she saw a round castle so high that she could not see to the top. And a star appeared above it with the most brilliant golden light, which illuminated the world like the sun. From that star emanated a distinctly glistening beam. That castle was very beautifully located, since it was on a high mountain, and before the castle in the valley was a spacious green meadow, through which ran a fast-flowing river, quite broad, not deep, so that it was possible to wade through it, transparent and very clear. Next to the river rested an infinite number of human beings, as those who are on a journey and intend to continue their journey by foot are accustomed. And all these seemed to belong to that castle. And she recognized all of them, even those whom she had not seen before. They were all the religious in orders or the religious who lived in the world.

The castle walls were made of square-cut stones of a very white color mixed with a little red. In a certain area, the wall was [*sic*] and appeared a little dark, in another very bright and shiny, and so different areas characterized the wall. At some point a rather thick fog surrounded the wall. When the star's light became stronger than the fog, the star chased it away, and then the castle's brightness was immense. In the castle were two iron portals, both closed, and one built close to the other. All of this was explained to her by the divine voice.

The castle represents any just person, with whom one takes refuge during times of affliction, as in a castle. And she gave the example of the duchess and the Viennese people who fled to the assistance of the just during the time of tribulation caused by the Hungarians and infidels. The Divine voice also said about the star, "That star is the road of understanding Divine goodness." Hearing this made her very happy, because much was shown to her in the vision a short time ago, which she could not fully understand. Therefore she hoped that she would be taught in the light of the star. And behold! Soon a large cluster of shimmering jewels appeared to her, in which the radiant light of the star was doubled in brilliance. And the voice said to her, "Look at these jewels! Their brightness caught your eye, but you do not know their true name and their powers, much as you cannot describe all that you have seen so that someone else can understand it."

She said about the beam that emanated from the star, "This is the light and the fire of Divine love, in which the soul becomes enraptured beyond itself and is lifted up above itself into the origin of the first creation. And this happens for three reasons. First, because God is delighted that the being created in His image, existing in such a fragile body and prison, is worthy of such exquisite grace. Second, because God wishes that His miracles and the secrets of His wisdom be revealed regarding what has happened and what will happen. Third, because God wishes that His creature, that is the rational soul, would improve herself so that those who are lax become aroused in Divine love.

"The first are, so to speak, the sons loved by God, and God is close to them, and they can never fall through a mortal sin; they are so anchored in grace, and whatever they ask, they receive [from God]. The second are human beings small in faith and trust and caught up in confusion. The Lord consoles and strengthens them in this way [i.e. through rapture]. And those are the ones appointed for a limited time only, such as the prelates of the Franciscans, who are now exalted, now deposed. The third are lax people who the Lord improves through His visitation. Those who lapse after having received such great grace, rarely or never rise up again.

"In the castle already mentioned were two iron portals, both closed, one built close to the other. A closed portal made of iron signifies the firm guard of the inner and outer senses of the just, so that no access to the soul is open to a mortal sin. The other portal signifies the guard of those around us, which they strengthen with good examples and doctrine. That the castle wall was, however, darkened in some places and shiny in others signifies that no matter how perfect someone is and how shining in virtues, he still has the darkness of imperfection mixed into this life.

"That thick fog surrounded the castle at some point, however, and that at another time the light of the star chased the fog away, signify that tribulations and temptations often surround the just, which they nonetheless overcome and vanquish through beneficial grace."

Chapter 131. Regarding the Elevation of Christ through Several [Priests] at the Same Time

And when she was in this vision, a thought about the Lord's Body occurred to her in her heart [about] that and when It was lifted up simultaneously by several [priests]. The Divine voice responded to her thought and said, "As in the Incarnation, the Son of God came from the Father's heart into the Virgin's womb to become flesh, so in the hour of immolation, He comes into the hand of every priest."

Likewise, she wondered whether He was equally powerful in heaven and in the sacrament. The Divine voice answered, "His power radiates more in heaven, but His gentleness shines in the sacrament, because He is with as much gentleness in the sacrament of the altar as He was with the ox and the donkey in the manger." And the Lord added, "He is harshly present to those who do not venerate or honor Him as God." This statement concerns mostly the bad priests, who most of the time die a difficult death and [have] a miserable end.

And because the Divine voice said to her above that the soul is sometimes enraptured beyond herself, the voice explained this statement and said, "Not all are enraptured in a perfect rapture like Blessed Paul and Blessed John. Others, however, become enraptured in a certain flow of Divine light, where often Divine secrets are revealed to them as the Lord wills it." Then she thought about her rapture and the revelation of the first vision of this little work. The Divine voice responded to this thought and said, "If a vision of God reached the power of mind or the reflectivity of the soul[68] only through a very small eyelet, as big as the eye of a needle, the soul could see and understand everything that exists in God."

Chapter 132. Regarding Naked Monks[69]

One morning after Matins the hand of the Lord came over her, and she saw in a vision completely naked men, and they were religious [i.e. members of a religious order, possibly Franciscans]. And she was given to understand that they were religious who, although they should have edified those around them through their example, influenced them badly through their loose manners. And as was given her

---

68 *visio Dei ad mentis aciem vel contuitum animae perveniret.*
69 In Blannbekin's spiritual world, nudity can have both negative and positive connotations, depending on the context. This vision must have been somewhat risqué, since the scribe emphasizes in the following chapter that it did *not* take place in church, but at home. The Franciscan *locus classicus* for positively encoded male nudity is of course St. Francis's public undressing in order to "follow nakedly the naked Christ" (*nudus nudum sequi*). See Thomas of Celano, *Vita prima*, c. 15 (*Fontes Franciscani*, edited and translated by Fausta Casolim [Assisi: Edizioni Porziuncola, 1997]). If this and the following vision are placed in a Franciscan context, they can be read as an implicit criticism of the order's acculturation into the medieval religious "mainstream". For a more unambiguously positive example of male nudity, in this case Christ, see chapters 140, 141, 154, 215; for a perhaps positive vision of both a friar and virgins in the nude, see chapters 227 and 228, although it is possible that this vision was written tongue in cheek.

to understand, those were not criminals, but so reckless in jokes and stupidities that although they [i.e. jokes] might have occurred sometimes without mortal sin, nonetheless [they] are more reprehensible among the religious and deprive them of grace and merit, which are withdrawn from them. Those [monks] actually become less fit for grace.

Chapter 133. Regarding a Group of Religious who Are Indignant about the Shortcomings of Others

This vision [above] happened at home in her prayer cell. When she then came to church in the morning during Mass, while in ecstasy, she saw a group of religious in very beautiful and colorful dress who were surrounded by an immense light, and they shimmered, but their eyes were bandaged and wrapped with cloth. Also, the embellishments of the garments, which were huge, drooped a bit. And it was given her to understand that they were the religious who, while leading a good life, were indignant about the shortcomings of others or about others because of their shortcomings and sins more than was appropriate. And because they showed themselves off in their good deeds more than necessary and worried about being recognized by others, they were impeded by this in the light of grace and Divine understanding.

Chapter 134. Regarding the Merits of the Church in Cooperation

Then, on the same day, she heard one Mass around the third hour. And as she came into the spirit during Mass, she saw these and those, that is the naked and those with bandaged eyes, to the left of the priest who read Mass. To his right, however, she saw many others dressed luminously and in white. And they all made a pile as if working together, so that different people threw different things onto the heap, which was big and high and very bright. And the priest himself who read Mass also helped to stack it.

Some carried a crystal rock in which the sun radiated in immense light. Others carried a backpack filled with goods. Some brought purest gold, others different kinds of precious gems. Some colorful and valuable cloth, some most plentiful light that gave light to all others. Some carried a bundle on their shoulders that all others supported with their hands; others appeared full of eyes. Yet on top of the heap stood a person who in herself was more exquisite and beautiful than all others. She existed in everyone in a complete way. Her light shone back [from everyone] and she adorned their beauty.

It was given to her to understand this vision: the heap represents the merits of the Church as a [harmonious] community. In the solar crystal, humility is signified; compassion in the backpack filled with goods; in the purest gold patience in the face of contempt; in the valuable and colorful jewels patience during hardships and suffering; in the colorful and valuable cloth patience in the face of injustice or violence.

Purity is symbolized through the most plentiful light, which gave light to others. Voluntary poverty is represented in the bundle carried on the shoulder. Joyful obedience is signified through those who appeared full of eyes, because the eyes of the Lord rest upon them. Love of God, or Charity, is symbolized by that singular person, more beautiful than all others and standing on the top of the heap, who is in all other virtues and forms them.

Chapter 135. Regarding the Arrival of Grace in the Soul

Another time, when she prayed in church, she felt a renewal of the spirit and a change in her heart, so that in the fire of devotion the blood of her lower body was drawn back to the heart. And she could not keep silent about what was in her heart, and even had to pronounce it loudly. She was truly astonished about this. Then, as she was accustomed, she visited daily the doorsteps of numerous churches. And when she was in the church of St. Jacob, she heard the voice within her say, "The grace that reaches the soul sets her on fire; the burning soul flows into the blood and sets it on fire. It gathers in the heart, the seat of life. And so the blood accomplishes five things in the body, namely to invigorate, to warm, to make happy, to form the ability to taste, and to make someone sleep sweetly.

"In the same way, grace causes and accomplishes these five things in the soul in a spiritual manner. First, she strengthens the soul so that she is able to achieve great and difficult matters in the service of God, even with a sometimes weak body. Second, it warms and ignites the soul with the fire of devotion and divine love. Such spiritual heat in the soul, mediated through the soul [to the body], sometimes acts in the body and tenses it. Third, she gladdens the soul and carries it into spiritual joy so that she feels neither sadness nor hostility, neither fear nor pain.

"And so she remains suspended and steady in joy as long as it pleases the Giver of Grace, so that the soul is not filled with anything else during that period of time. Fourth, she causes the soul to taste how sweet and lovely the Lord is, so that sometimes that sweetness and loveliness flows over into the bodily senses. Fifth, she causes the soul to sleep when through a secret causation of divine grace, the soul is carried away in ecstasy, outwardly sleeping and without sensation, [and] resting yet alert. Hence the saying: 'I am sleeping, but my heart is awake.' "[70]

Chapter 136. Regarding a Certain Spherical Light, in which She Saw Paradise with the Earth and Purgatory

On the day of the Lord's Resurrection, when she took communion, the hand of the Lord came over her, and she was in the spirit the whole day until the middle of the following night. Her spirit was carried away into a certain spherical light, which she believed to be the physical sun, but this was not so. For, as she was taught later on, it was not the sun, but a certain Divine light. It was an immense and extremely bright light equal in weight to the sun, and that light was directed towards east. And she was placed in the light and led along with the light. And she traveled above a pleasant place planted heavily with trees, and filled with many different delicious fruit. This was the area where God placed the first human being, as she was taught later on.

Then, guided in the light, she saw in one swoop the earth below, the whole world, its center and its surroundings. And the earth was round like a globe, and in regard to its surroundings, the earth barely seemed as big as an apple. And it seemed dark and not pleasant to look at and rather unsightly in comparison to the bright surroundings.

And so she was also led underneath the earth to nice enough places, where a large group of shimmering human beings with adorned faces appeared who, like mutes, did not speak. As she was taught later on, these were the dead who had died without grave sins. They did not receive any other punishment than the lack of the vision of God. But as she herself said, this punishment was the worst to them.

[70] See Song of Songs 5:2.

Chapter 137. Regarding the Trinity, the Wounds of Christ, Angels and All Created Beings, and the Dwellings of the Saints in the Fatherland

Led in this light, she then saw the heavenly city. And the light illumined this also for her, and all that she saw, she saw in this light. "We shall see the light in your light."[71] And so she saw God and recognized the most beautiful Trinity more distinctly than in any other vision. She told me some things about this that I could not grasp intellectually,[72] and she said that she knew and remembered several things intellectually, which she could not divulge publicly. She said that the wounds of the Savior and His humanity are the occasion for unspeakable joy for all in the fatherland, for angels as well as for human beings, and that the Savior was so friendly and close to the saints that it could not be explained [in words].

She also said that the holy angels and the souls of the just praise God and are glad to praise [Him] with such fervor that they can never get enough. All created beings, even those without rationality,[73] the elements and those composed of the elements, praise God in such harmony that even rational created beings in the fatherland are moved to praise God more [intensely].

She saw and recognized the dwellings of individuals in the fatherland, and of all those still existing in mortal flesh. And remaining in the already mentioned light, she discerned all human beings.

Chapter 138. Regarding Patience and Two Types of Devout Persons

She also said that it is of great merit before God to suffer in this world because of God. She also said that devotion pulls a person to God. She also saw two types of devout persons. Some are intent on devotion but are frequently sluggish and do not suffer many inconveniences. Others are intent on devotion, yet [engage in it] with pious efforts and acts of devotion performed in [the name of] God, and sufferings endured for the sake of God. The first are like those lying down. The Lord is with them now, and then again distant from them, because they cannot remain continuously connected with God through devotion. The others, however, continuously adhere to God and lean on Him. The first sometimes fall away from the Lord,

---

71 See Psalm 36:9.
72 *intellectu capere non potui.*
73 *omnis creatura, etiam irrationalis.*

affected by too much sluggishness. The others are a great example to people and of great merit before God.

Chapter 139. Regarding Certain Widows

When the soul had returned to the body, the body was so completely exhausted that she could feel it for several days. A certain devout person talked to me in a similar fashion. She was carried away in a vision to a lovely dwelling where there was a large group of women in white garments. And one among them said that all were once widows. That person also was a widow. When she asked to be permitted to remain with them, she was told, "You cannot now be here with us, but you must return to the body and suffer much in it. But afterwards, you will be with us." She then returned to the body and found the body so weak that she languished greatly for several weeks. Something similar can be read in Daniel 10 [*sic*], "I saw this great vision, and no strength remained within me, but my physique was changed; I became weak and had no vigor left."

Chapter 140. Regarding the Sidewound of Christ and Humility

On the fifth day after the first Sunday after Easter, when she was present at the Church service, an extremely beautiful man appeared to her in a vision, a well grown young man, completely naked and surrounded by immense light. She felt neither horror nor displeasure in seeing the shape and nudity of all his limbs, but rather was filled with a consolation of the spirit, as in other visions. His looks were desirable through and through, and He had his hands crossed over His chest, and under the right arm, a large and wide open wound appeared, in which fresh blood boiled like a hot pot bubbling by the fire, yet without flowing over. Nonetheless, the vision of this wound and this blood flow did not instill in her either fear or horror, as happens at the sight of bleeding mortal human beings, but the sight of this wound brought her rather joy of the spirit.

The Lord also said, "I am prepared to offer Myself to all who are desiring and sustaining Me with humility." Yet when these things happened, a certain priest, who wished to celebrate Mass, elevated the Body of the Lord. Then a certain devout person, who wanted to invite her to look at the Body of the Lord, nudged her at the wrong moment, and so the Lord disappeared from her eyes. Yet that virgin told me that it would not be necessary to poke her when she had a vision during Mass, because the Lord permits her always to come back to herself to such a degree that she can see the Body of the Lord.

On the following day, a Friday, when a certain religious preached to some nuns in a monastery, this virgin was present as well. And when she concentrated on the face of the preacher with the desire to hear the word of God, the hand of the Lord came upon her there, and the Lord appeared to her again as on the day before, naked and with hands folded across His chest, and with boiling blood in the wound of the side. And He turned back and forth several times between the virgin and the preaching friar, yet without speaking anything.

Chapter 141. Regarding a Devout Sermon and the Side Wound

A little while later, on the feast day of St. George, when she heard again the word of God in the same church, the hand of the Lord came upon her. And Christ appeared to her completely naked and with His hands crossed over His chest, and the wound below His right arm open wide and with the blood bubbling as in the previous visions. The Lord Himself spoke all the words of the preacher. And this vision lasted for a while, and then she came back to herself while the preacher was still speaking and preaching. And when the friar dealt with the passage from the Song of Songs, "The King has led me into His chamber",[74] she came again into the spirit, and the Lord appeared to her naked and wounded as before. And the Lord said to her, "When a preacher proclaims the word of God with devotion and to praise God, then God is present in his mouth and speaks through his mouth, because someone preaching like this will be lifted up in God."

For this reason, the Lord spoke the preacher's words [in her vision].

Chapter 142 and 143. Regarding a Certain Beguine who Lived in Worldly Comfort and Regarding the Devil's Cunning

This virgin had a female companion, also a virgin of great holiness, who was introduced to the Duchess because of her holiness. This lady took her into her household and cared for her most tenderly, for she had been ill for a long time. This virgin was told how the Duchess was of one mind with her companion and how the whole household desired her favors and cared for her magnificently.

Now this virgin found such honor and favor suspicious, and when she was by herself, she thought in her heart, "O God, how are things with my companion?" Soon she came into the spirit and heard the

---

[74] See Song of Songs 1:4.

voice within say to her, "As the king who triumphed over the enemy and killed the king carried the banner of the Holy Cross in glory to Jerusalem, and upon arrival at the city was forbidden to enter, the wall and gate closed by Divine order, so the gate and access to grace, which the Lord was used to visit upon her, will be closed before her, if she will continue to remain in that comfort and renown. For the Lord has shown Himself so intimately to her in her inner self and poured into her such tenderness of comfort and grace during all tribulation caused by her illness and deprivation because she had carried her cross for so long and so continually. Now, because she entrusted herself into hands who ought not to know the secrets of Divine comfort, therefore the portals of grace are closed before her."

Then she became frightened and thought, "O Lord, will she therefore fall into sin?" The Lord said to her, "No, but the usual grace will be withdrawn from her." And the Lord added, "The Devil, because he could not block [out] grace in her during [times] of deprivation and illness, was jealous of so much grace. He tried, as much as he could, that she would receive much comfort and honor in [the world of] time, so that he could achieve through prosperity what he could not accomplish in adversity."

Chapter 144. Regarding Humility, Grace, and Desire

On the following day, when she had taken communion, she thought about her companion, who was so ensnared by the devil's cunning, and she said in her heart, "O God, what should a person do?" The Lord said to her, "Nothing will be able to ensure grace as much as a person always remaining humble, not only within, but also through outward behavior, so that he may as much as possible remain hidden in his good deeds." She, however, thought in her heart as follows. "O Lord, people are edified through good examples." The Lord answered, "The more they hide, the more they edify." The Lord also said that a person should not rejoice over a spiritual consolation, if he does not progress through it in grace. And the Lord added, "A person can neither work for nor grow toward grace through continuous physical efforts. And therefore he should always stay in a mental state of desire for an increase in grace, and in this, he makes progress. And whenever desire quiets down, then progress in grace quiets down, and when desire decreases, so does grace."

Likewise, she was told that the above mentioned companion was clothed with the valuable dresses of the Duchess herself and that she liked this and all embellishment a lot. For she was used to draw interior devotion from external beauty. That virgin [Agnes] recognized this well, and when she was by herself, she began to think about her companion with some ambivalence, because she engaged in this [her behavior] with great sincerity. Then the interior voice said to her, "The devil has blinded her in this, because she enjoys it."

God also said that she would not escape punishment for this.

*   *   *75

Chapter 153. Regarding the Magical Treatment of the Body of Christ

On the Friday after the Day of Ascension of the Lord, when she was in church after Compline, a countrywoman, it seemed, with covered face, came to her and said that the Body of the Lord seemed to lie [exposed] on the altar. And this rural woman pressured the virgin to show it to a priest. That peasant woman was suspected to have placed the Body of the Lord [there]. The devout [virgin] went and as she saw a part of the host [lying there], she became very alarmed. She began to wonder whether it was a consecrated host or not. And when she kneeled there before the altar, she soon felt a spirit of consolation, and her doubts left her. Yet when she got up again, she began again to doubt whether it was the Body of the Lord or not. And that mental conflict was very painful.

And whenever she got up, that temptation assaulted her, and when she bent her knees, it left her. Finally, the friar sacristan joined her, to whom she showed the host. He kept it for the next day to take it with reverence because of the doubt. This devout woman began also to think about the Body of the Lord, whether it would be and remain the Body of the Lord if it were handled irreverently by sorcerers. Divine inspiration within her answered, "If feet trample on the body of the Lord, no foot or shoe can touch Him, nor can He suffer anything, even if He is thrown into a cesspool, because due to the Passion, He became unable to suffer once and for all."

Chapter 154. Regarding the Lamb Clothed in Flesh

Later in the evening, when she was in the prayer cell in her house after her Compline, she came into the spirit. And behold, a lamb

---

75 Chapters 145–52 discuss gradations and classifications of virtuous behavior and spiritual treasures, such as the seven steps of compassion, the triple grading of patience, the quintuple path of poverty, the merits of the just, etc.

appeared to her, big like a one year old calf, clothed in human flesh, naked, with a human face, and walking on four feet like a lamb, the face turned toward the earth, and a diadem around its head. During this apparition, she became confused, and soon the vision disappeared, and she came to herself again. And after a little while, the lamb appeared to her again, as it had appeared before, and again disappeared. And there she received the spirit of consolation and the fire of love.

Yet when she went to church on the following day, a Saturday, several Masses were read there simultaneously. Hearing them always gave her much grace and devotion, and she wished to apply herself to devotions, because it was her habit that she frequently conducted her own meditations. Coming into the spirit, she saw a lamb white as snow, with whitest wool. The lamb, however, was of medium size. It walked around all the altars where Masses were read, and kissed with its mouth the chasubles of all priests, perambulating happily. She, however, was suffused with great wonder.

And behold, suddenly she found the lamb standing next to her, kissing her cheeks. The contact with it filled her with sweet fire, even physically. At that moment, a priest who celebrated a Mass intended to lift the Body of the Lord. Interrupted by a certain person to look at the Body of the Lord, she became so perturbed that the vision disappeared. After the elevation of the Body of Christ, however, she again dedicated herself to the serenity of contemplation. And suddenly, coming into the spirit, she found the lamb next to her just as before, and it seemed to her as if she inclined herself toward the lamb and said to it, commending it in her heart, "O Beloved, did You come to us as well?" And the little lamb said, "I give Myself to the priests, and they offer Me to the Father. And I have smelled the odor of the sweetness of their devotion walking around each of them. Other persons dedicated to contemplation as well attract Me to them and keep Me close to them so that I neither can nor want to leave them."

Chapter 155. Learn Here about the Lamb and about Fortune-Tellers and Sorcerers

Then she said in her heart, "O Lord, what does it mean that You appeared to me with such a sad appearance?" The little lamb answered, "I appeared to you twice as a lamb of the size of a one year old calf, first, because I was slaughtered like a calf. The calf does not die as easily as a lamb, because the calf is stronger than a lamb. I was slaughtered in such great pain and with such a hard death, but many ponder my death only rarely. Secondly, because cattle are herded and are in the power of him who herds them, and do not resist him. So I am in the power of all, whether sinners or the just, who herd Me like the cattle to the stable. This is what the sinners do: they herd Me, I say, where they want to, not where I want [to go] – those such as fortune-tellers, sorcerers, and other criminals. But now I am appearing joyfully because of the smell of the devotions of good people."

This vision occurred in the morning, when Masses were read in the church of the friars.

But around the third hour, a certain friar read Mass. She was present and came into the spirit at the hour of immolation and saw a little lamb, very white, standing on the paten before the officiating, that entered into the mouth of the priest. And all good people and she also received that little lamb. She greatly wondered, however, that the priests, who received that lamb while officiating by themselves, did not receive less [of it] with the others the second time. And she said that the friars, who ate it, were perhaps preparing to go to the precincts. Those who were at breakfast during that hour received that blessed lamb together with the officiating priest. And she said that without knowing it, those who received the lamb obtained exceedingly great strength against sin and against the propensity to sin.

Chapter 156. Regarding Priests who do not Receive the Lamb

When Mass was completed, she went to another church. For it was her habit to visit churches as long as she could hope that a Mass was celebrated somewhere. And she came upon a priest reading Mass, and at the hour of sacrifice, she came into the spirit again and again saw the little lamb standing on the paten as she had seen it during the previous Mass. But it was not granted to that priest to receive the lamb, but other good people and [people] well prepared for the meal of the lamb, who were indeed without mortal sin, received this lamb.

And she gave the parable of the Savior as an example, where a man prepared a large meal and invited many who failed to come and then the Lord ordered others to be invited to the meal.[76] So, if a priest

---

[76] See Luke 14:16–24.

is careless and unworthy, the Lord for that reason does not suffer that the fruit of that most holy sacramental meal will perish.

Chapter 157. Regarding Those who Are Tumultuous and Quarrelsome in the World

On the day of Pentecost, when she had taken communion, the hand of the Lord came upon her around the third hour, and she saw a light much like the light of a very large candle. In this light [was] the whole world, kings and princes and the powerful of the world, the laity as well as clerics, disorderly and quarrelsome against each other and amongst themselves. And it seemed a great muddle, so that she herself became flustered seeing this. And in her mind, she tried to renounce the vision as much as she could. She also understood that as the light of a candle burning down is reduced to ashes and dust, so the people of the world fight over temporal goods and over honors, which are compared to ashes and dust.

Chapter 158. Regarding the Holy Spirit and the Parisian Chapter of the Friars[77]

Afterwards, she was carried into the light and something like the brilliancy of heaven and was lifted up high like an eagle so that she could see all that was in the world. Also at that time, the general chapter of the Franciscans was held in Paris, and she herself saw the friars congregated as one and many [of them were] in the choir at Mass. She also described to me the layout of the church and the altar as I have heard elsewhere from those who had been there. During Mass then, when the Mass of the Holy Spirit was sung, a huge flame descended among the friars, and widely dispersed sparks appeared among the friars, and all who were present there received the Holy Spirit in such abundance, as she herself recognized, that all were strengthened in grace.

Lifted up in the light in such fashion, she saw the orb of the world filled with the spirit of the Lord and the Holy Spirit influencing various virtues among human beings. And some were richer in

---

[77] Possibly the Chapter of 1292, which is known mainly because of its condemnation of the teachings of Peter John Olivi. See Dinzelbacher, "Die Wiener Minoriten", 187. If this Chapter is the correct one, we may assume that events of the *vita* were placed in the text with some disregard as to their temporal occurrence. Chapter 189, for example, explicitly mentions the year 1291.

virtues than others. She told me about some virtues, as I will report below. She recognized all virtues, however, and said that each virtue can be recognized through a light that is distinct from the others.

Chapter 159. Regarding Love, [and] what it can Gain as Merit

Regarding love, she also mentioned in particular that although all light flows from God, love itself is before all others merged into the light that is God. All other virtues are illumined through the light of love, and she said that this is the highest. And she said that through the movement of love, more would be merited than through mourning, flagellation, and similar efforts, since something venial is forgiven; also, when someone is in the motion and act of love, he is cleansed in the fire of love. She said that the devout that languish and are as if weakened in the love of God, God, Love, holds in His hands, protects, and embraces. And those devout souls certainly lean on Him even more.

She also said that if she was meant to live for thirty more years, it would be barely long enough to talk about all that she recognized regarding virtues and other matters, if it were possible to explain all of this in a conversation or to be grasped by human intellect.[78] Inasmuch as someone born blind can neither grasp nor understand what someone tells him about the appearance of the sun and its beauty, so the human intellect, if not illumined by Divine light, cannot understand the secret Divine words which are seen and heard in the spirit.

Chapter 160. Regarding Chastity and Those who Backslide

She said in regard to chastity that it is the gateway to and foundation of all virtues. And that God loved her most tenderly and that she is on most intimate terms with God and that a brightness reflected from her much like the light of Christ's humanity, similar to love in the Divine light, and most of all to virginal chastity.

She also said, "He gladly and promptly obeys those who for the sake of God guard their intact virginal chastity. Their wishes, so to speak, command the Lord, and He receives the risk of their act of requesting more with grace – more so than [the wishes] of those who once had stained their innocence, even if they might have done penitence later." And she said that the sin [of those who backslide] affects most of all a soul alienated from the Holy Spirit. And the Holy Spirit's access to their hearts is more difficult than to other sinners.

---

78   *ab intellectu humano capi.*

And as often as they are contrite and [yet] backslide again, and lapse so frequently after the grace of compunction, so do they close and obstruct as if with a bulwark and a bolt the gate of grace before them and become more inhospitable to grace.

She also said that those who grow old in this sin, that is, incontinence, rarely or never mend their ways. And that even good married couples living without mortal sin, however much they may be in grace, nonetheless never receive new grace while they are in [the midst of] the conjugal act.

Chapters 161, 162, 163, 164. Regarding the Degrees of Humility, Patience, Fear, Obedience, and the Work of the Holy Spirit

Humility is the greatest trader[79] of grace and merits, and she kindles the light of love, and love submits to her in her works. Relevant to humility is that first, she is humble in herself, not wise beyond herself. Secondly, she sets an example to those around her; thirdly, she is kind and gentle in her actions; fourthly, she is compliant with those around her; fifthly, she is pleasant before God and receives God's blessings with devout acts of thanksgiving. And when she feels herself to receive any kind of Divine grace, she lowers herself even more and recognizes what comes from herself. Compassion is of such great merit that it recompenses God for the benefaction of the Passion and Death [of Christ]. Patience follows the Lord in the form of a little lamb and gathers much fruit. Therefore demons are extremely happy when they can cause any good people to be impatient. Patience is like a carrier of a light that removes and extinguishes impatience. Fear is the guard of virtues and graces and like a gatekeeper who does not permit anything pernicious to invade the soul.

Obedience is even more meritorious, because it abnegates one's own will and is always in the act of gaining merit. What for another would not be a merit sometimes or only a small merit, for him who is obedient it is always a greater merit, and he always ascends to God continuously as if step after step. As to the most faithful, the Lord has committed to him precious treasures[80] to guard.

She said that the Holy Spirit operates in all those baptized, even in

---

79 *negotiatrix.* Note the feminine gender; I have kept it for the remainder of the chapter.

80 The scribe uses only a Middle High German word for "treasures", *cleynodia*, instead of a Latin term. Usually, he offers both a Latin term and a Middle High German word as its translation.

sinners, because the seal of the Holy Spirit is impressed upon them through Him [Holy Spirit]. Therefore He does not abandon them anywhere. In the sinner, He works either a change of heart [i.e. conversion] or protects the sinner much like a shield, so that the devil cannot throw him into every evil that he intends.

She saw the unbelievers, however, and the non-baptized as if in a dark dungeon and in one heap. They did not seem to have life, expecting [the moment] when the earth would open its gullet and devouring them into the depths. She saw good people receive the Holy Spirit sevenfold. Some received [Him] in fire through the kindling of Divine love, some in the voice of the praise of God's word, some in a storm through compunction and the pain of sins, some in the sweet dew of spiritual consolation or through the spiritual consolation of despondency, others in a certain light through internal revelation, through which they contemplate Divine secrets, internally consumed and enraptured [by the light]. This, however, happens only to few. Others [received Him] in the form of a dove through gentleness and mildness of spirit and through a simplicity of heart. Others received the Holy Spirit in the manna of hidden sweetness.

Chapter 165. Regarding Christ's Gifts

On the feast of the Holy Trinity, Christ appeared to her clothed in priestly garments except for the chasuble. He came to congregate all the elect before the Father so that as the Father takes pleasure in His only-begotten and coeternal Son, so He might find pleasure in all of His elect. And whatever they lack in merits for His satisfaction, the Son of God Himself supplements through the merits of His Passion and Death.

Also, a countless multitude of human beings appeared to her there, huddling together. Christ, however, gave each person a gift from His hand. However much He gave, His right hand nonetheless always remained filled. He did not have less in His hand to give because of this. Although He gave different gifts, all were shining bright and distinctive in their type of luminosity. She explained to me some of these gifts.

Some shone in white light, and they signify chastity. Some gleamed in the color of heaven, and they signify the holiness of an exemplary life. And she said that it is of greater merit to convert one sinner through a good example than a hundred through a sermon.

Others were red and signify mortification [of the flesh] and physical suffering. Others were green and signify the greening of devotion and the uplifting of the mind in God through grace.[81] Others were of a golden light and signify love and charity.

Chapter 166. Regarding Negligence

On the day of St. Anthony, when she wished to take communion, she believed that her confessor, who used to offer her communion, intended to celebrate Mass in the monastery of St. Jacob. He had promised to preach there in the morning. She went to the said monastery. Her confessor, however, did not know [this], believing that she was in the church of the friars. There he read Mass and intended to offer her communion; she did not appear. And so, with communion neglected, she became very sad. Finally, she returned to the church of the friars around the hour and found someone willing to read Mass. And pulling herself together, she asked in [light of] this said offence to receive communion from him. And there, during Mass, she began to think through which sin had she deserved this confusion. And she received the answer, that she had deferred confession and communion for so long for [only] a slight reason. Her confessor had been away for a good eight days and in the meantime she had neglected to confess to someone else and to take communion, even though there was a feast day when other devout persons took communion. The Lord punished her for this negligence. And the Lord said to her, "Your confessor has also carried his punishment, that is the withdrawal of grace and spiritual visitation, because he neglected himself internally by exposing himself to the exertions of the journey and to external tasks."

Chapter 167. Regarding the Right Hand, which was Pierced by a Long Wound, and Regarding Patience

After a short while, during that Mass, she saw in her spirit a right hand, pierced with a long wound. She certainly felt the Lord, but could not see anything but the hand.

The Lord also laid the palm of His hand over her mouth and face, and from this contact she felt a marvelously fragrant odor and the fire of devotion and love in her heart. And she glowed from such

---

81 The concept of greening has been thoroughly investigated in regard to Hildegard of Bingen, who used this concept amply, although *viriditas* is already documented in Gregory the Great's homilies. See Margot Schmidt, op. cit., 386–87, for a full bibliographical discussion, including Barbara Newman's work. For another reference in Blannbekin's *vita*, see chapter 174.

ardor of desire that she could barely contain herself. She felt the fire from the contact with the wounded hand also physically in her face. Nonetheless, she received a most intensive consolation of the spirit and heard the Lord's voice say to her, "Learn patience in adversity and look how much I have suffered when I hung by my hands on the cross, since the nail tore such a long wound through the weight of the body pulling downwards."

When that virgin of Christ told me this, she could barely speak because of tears. This happened around the sixth hour on Friday, the day of St. Anthony. On Monday, however, after she had confessed and told me this, the flame of divine desire still burned in her chest. She told me that on the following day, the force of love and the ardor of desire had grown so much in her chest that she was unable to endure it and had almost begun to scream. But she pleaded with the Lord not to permit her to become the target of gossip, and the Lord prevented it.

On the following Saturday, after she had heard the sermon and seen some people devoutly receiving Holy Communion, she began to burn in a great desire for communion. And so she went to another church, where a certain monk, a devout man, purified his hand over the chalice after communion. And she desired to at least drink from the chalice, and approached [him]. And the monk, appreciating her devotion, offered her [a sip] from this purification, in which seemed to her to be something like a little crumb of the Lord's Body, which she ate joyfully and happily. Receiving this, she soon felt so much consolation of the spirit that she became rapt in great admiration for God's goodness.

And she heard a voice within her say to her, "Why do you marvel over my goodness? I can give more than a human being can receive. And my delight is to be with devout hearts and souls who desire me from the heart."

Chapter 168. Regarding Withdrawn Grace, through what It can be Recovered, and Regarding the Five Wounds

Then she went to the church of St. Stephen and wished to dedicate herself to contemplation, yet in her heart there was much thinking and worrying over how she abided by God. And she heard the voice within her that repeated to her what she had seen about the wounded hand. And the voice said, "A person who is unsettled by worries or from whom grace has been withdrawn can in nothing recover grace and find peace of heart as well as in the devout remembrance of Christ's Passion."

And it added, "In the right hand and wound, search for and learn patience, and how patiently the Son of God suffered, as you have seen His hand, lacerated by a wound. In the left hand learn and search humility, and how humbly the Son of God has suffered. In the wound of the right foot search for and draw out compassion, and [see] how He was merciful to the human race with great compassion. In the left foot, learn to suffer willingly and the desire to suffer. In the wound of [His] side, learn love, which the Bridegroom offered His bride, the Church, to drink from there. And He offered her love through the open side of the heart.

"Notice also the blood that flows from the side, which causes the fire of devotion in devout souls. Notice also the water flowing from the side, which signifies tears, with which devout souls are washed and cleansed. And nonetheless, the flow of this water signifies the flow of grace from God into the soul."

Chapter 169. Regarding Saint Peter's and Saint Paul's Complaints about a Certain Bishop

On the eighth day before the Feast of the Apostles, a Sunday, the Lord appeared to her clothed in priestly garments except for the chasuble, carrying a large axe on his shoulder, much larger than the one in another vision above.[82] However, He threatened the bishop with [his] demise. Namely, Blessed Peter and Blessed Paul, whose feast was impending at that time, raised a complaint about the bishop, that he had confounded the people of God by thrusting an all too indiscriminate interdict onto the whole diocese. But Blessed Stephen was present, the patron of the church in Passau, and asked and received for him an extension until the feast of Blessed Apostles Peter and Paul, that he might mend his ways. The virgin, however, wondered about this to herself, why the axe, which the Lord had raised against the Lord Bishop, was larger than that which He had raised against the king of the Romans, who was already dead in this year.[83] And it was given her to understand that because spiritual might is indeed greater than secular power, therefore this sentence is heavier and more [significant].

Blessed Peter was clothed in papal garments and the miter, and had in his hand the crosier [and was] dressed with a scarlet or red chasuble. Blessed Paul was clothed in white garments without the

---

[82] See chapter 85.
[83] I.e. Rudolf I of Habsburg, who died in 1291.

chasuble. Blessed Stephen was clothed with a completely red tunic that reached down to his feet.

The Bishop, however, stood far apart when this happened.

Chapter 170. Regarding the Reading in the Five Wounds of Christ

Likewise, the Crucified appeared to her, and in every wound one could read as if [there were] written letters. In the wound of the right hand, one could read, "I have bought you back from eternal death and I am a shield for you against all difficulties." In the wound of the left hand, one could read, "Flee securely to Me and do not distrust! I have indeed expended Myself greatly for you. Therefore those who mistrust Me sin more gravely than Judas did when he sold Me." In the wound of the right foot, one could read, "I am Myself the inflow of grace and the origin of goodness." In the wound of [His] side was written, "Enter all through this opening, who search to see the Divine face! And the more deeply you enter, the more clearly you will recognize the Divine."

This fivefold writing of the five wounds referred, however, to all Christians without distinction. Nonetheless, everybody read specifically in the same wounds of the Crucified one's own [message]. And she gave an example of one certain religious person, who read in the wound of the right hand, "I am ready for the mandate of obedience." In the left hand, he read the effort to know oneself. In the wound of the right foot, he read to search for nothing else and only to desire what could move him forward in God and join him with God. In the wound of the left foot, he read to desire from [the depths of] his heart to suffer death for Christ. In the wound of the side, he read always to desire the sweetness within and lasting consolation in the heart of God.

Chapter 171. Regarding the Withdrawal of Grace from the Confessor of this Virgin

At a certain time, I went around sadly because of the withdrawal of Divine grace. As if languishing in the spirit, I was not able to raise my heart toward celestial desire or to engage myself in feelings of devotion. Yet when I accepted this as if I suffered a rejection, all that was left of me was like dried wood. I also revealed my miseries to this virgin. Through her prayers, she came frequently to my support [when I was] in similar straits. And the Lord told her that this gloominess had happened because of my sins, that is because I had dedicated myself too much to reconcile the Lady Duchess regarding a certain turmoil which caused her to turn against the friars, and because I became too distracted due to the gravity and dignity of her . . . [role in the dispute? word/s missing in the manuscript].[84]

There was also another sin, and that is when I sang in the choir and should have been with God within, I was looking back and saw several [things] about which I had too much displeasure and indignation. I guessed well enough that the first sin was the cause of my desolation. The second I did not detect; but after she told me this, then I clearly recognized that I was exasperated during [the canonical] hours and impatiently rebuked a certain novice.

And when she told me all this, I saw my deficiency and misery, and asked her that she would appeal to God for me regarding my sorrows and that He would have compassion with me and would make me a good friar. She prayed, however, and received the following answer. "What do you ask for? If he wishes that nothing will harm him, then it is necessary that he becomes nothing." She, however, did not understand this word and wondered what it was all about, or in what way he ought to become nothing. And when she quietly ruminated about this in her heart, she heard the voice saying to her, "He should turn himself to nothing in such a way that he ought to be concerned above all about himself. He ought to watch over his improvement, rejecting and guarding himself against, that is not loving whatever may hinder his progress and improvement."

I believe that this meaning concurs with the words of the Savior in the gospel, "Who wants to make his soul whole should lose it, and who lost it because of me, shall make it whole."[85] The Lord also added, "That soul has delights who becomes saddened over its impairment, that is the soul's impairment."

I believe that this was also said because of her [i.e. Agnes]. She was at that time also sad, because she experienced Divine visitations less frequently. She became also often very disturbed over her mistakes, no matter how small.

---

[84] Possibly Elisabeth, the wife of Duke Albrecht I. The Viennese Franciscans were close to the nobility and the royal house of the Babenberger. See Dinzelbacher, "Die Wiener Minoriten", 182.

[85] See Luke 17:33.

Chapter 172. Regarding Two, which of Them God Loved More

It happened that three brothers, to whom she was especially well disposed, one day read Mass in succession before an altar, where she had taken communion that day. And it came to her in her heart, which of them God loved more. And soon she reprimanded herself, because this was an idle and superfluous thought. And so she became quiet and dedicated herself to contemplation. And the hand of the Lord came over her, and she came into the spirit and heard, "Behold, the Lord intends to do your will. God loves him who just read Mass tenderly and sweetly, because he preserved his virginal innocence. God does not permit him to suffer anything, much like a mother a child, whom she loves tenderly and cuddles and protects from adversity. And he, content with the grace bestowed upon him by God, thus is soothed in His love."

Then the Lord said again, "Friar Nicholas, who read Mass before him, is loved by God with strong love. And those that are in continuous struggle against the flesh and often triumphant, have much merit before God." And the Lord takes from those merits and places them in the communal treasures of the Church. And there are very few who do not fall into evil thoughts by sometimes not resisting or denouncing [them] strongly. Whenever, through evil angels, insinuations of bad thoughts happen and are not resisted with the necessary denunciation, then the legion, that is, the multitude of demons, rejoices, hoping that through this they can advance themselves some more. For that reason, they continue on with their attacks. Therefore it happens that for many, this struggle extends into old age.

Chapter 173. What for God Is the Most Gratifying about a Human Being

Actually, God loves the third friar, who first read Mass, with fervent love. Therefore he is often fiery in devotion and keeps burning towards God in grace and virtues. Those, however, have the best part of love; the reason being that God is pleased by this the most. That is if someone burns like this in the love of God and fervently desires God and His gifts: this is the most gratifying to God. Those shine with good examples before people. Of course, the more they thirst for God and God's grace within, the less they allow for any frivolity, but, always serious and mature, they present a good example to their fellow humans and teach by example. Therefore they partake in the reward for preachers. These also have a strong determination to endure for the sake of God, and in this they merit the reward [reserved] for martyrs. And because they always languish in desire for God, they are received in the abyss of Divine light, that is, the cognition of God, and are led before all others into the lusciousness of Divine sweetness.

Chapter 174. Regarding a Rainbow and Conversations with God

In those days, once again the hand of the Lord came upon her, [and] she came into the spirit. And a rainbow appeared to her, in which the sun was reflected, from the opposite side. And she was told by the voice within, "The arc represents the soul, the blue or pale color represents humility, which attracts grace to the soul, much like the most water is attracted in that part of the rainbow. The green color signifies the greening of grace, through which the soul greens in God and which makes a place for God in the soul. The red color represents the fire of divine love in the soul. The dark or earthy color signifies the effort of freely chosen works and suffering for God."

And after this it was shown to her that the arc was placed before her across the earth. And she saw writing in it and read, "Whenever you are [plural] engaged in conversations about God and do not feel these four things in the soul, then be afraid that you have said something insolent, which [causes] you to not feel grace."

Chapter 175. Regarding Kissing the Altar and a Sweetness Similar to a Warm Roll

During these days, it happened that she kissed the cloth of the altar on which Mass had been celebrated that day. Out of devotion, she was actually used to doing this every day. In this kiss, the Lord gave her devotion the consolation that always, when she kissed the altar when on that particular day Mass was read, she felt a miraculous sweet scent similar to a warm [freshly baked] roll. Yet that sweetness surpassed without comparison the smell of a roll. The reason was that because of the scent of this sweetness, she felt the most luscious transformation in her spirit.

When she thus covered the altar [with kisses], she saw something like a drop, and in the belief that it was a tear of devotion shed by the priest, who just had celebrated Mass there [and] for whom she had special grace, she became happy about the drop and kissed it. But she felt nothing of the lusciousness of the usual scent. And soon, she became sad and went to another altar. When she kissed it everywhere, she received the usual sweetness. She also wondered what the reasons were for this, and the voice said to her, "This is happening, because you ought to know that this is only given by God. Do not hope to find this consolation anywhere else and do not expect to feel anything caused by the sanctity of the celebrant."

Chapter 176. Regarding an Unexpected [Act of] Grace

On the vigil of Saint Jacob, the Lord deigned to visit upon her even more copious grace and consolation so that she marveled that without any preparation, she had received such an abundance of sweetness and that she often labored harder in the fervor of devotion, [yet] received less. And the voice said to her, "As clouds filled abundantly pour rain on the earth, so the Lord, full of grace and goodness, confers grace in abundance so that His goodness becomes known to human beings. And when He has withdrawn Himself from humans at one hour, then a person thirsts more fervently to desire grace, which he had so abundantly before. And the Lord often pours an abundance of such sweetness unexpectedly so that a human being learns to ascribe nothing to his own powers, but only to God's gratuitous goodness."

Chapter 177. Regarding the Grace Received by a Certain Friar, the Soul, and the Three Things Brought Back after Rapture

One day, when she had taken communion, she came to the church of Saint Stephen, before the monstrance where the Body of the Lord is kept. Prostrating herself, she began to pray and adore [the Lord]. And soon, she came into the spirit, filled with not a little Divine consolation, and heard the voice within speak to her, "Demand what you will, and you will be granted [your wish]." And soon, [the thought of] a certain friar came into her heart, who had asked her to intercede on his behalf before the Lord, for the Lord to make him a good friar. And soon she prayed to the Lord from the heart and in the heart that He, according to His own discretion, would make her friend a good Franciscan friar.

The Lord said to her, "Demand for him one more thing, that is that the Lord may preserve him in all perfection!" She soon asked Him this not with [her] mouth, but with her heart's desire. And she received the answer that she was given a favorable hearing. And the Lord added, "I give you this as a sign that your wish has been granted: namely that the next three times that you take communion again, you will enjoy the blessing of Divine sweetness with abundance, so that not only will the Lord give Himself to you, but you will also be enraptured with all your soul." This actually happened.

And she said, "The soul brings three things with her after such rapture: first, a certain noble indignation and contempt against all that is worldly, and disgust against all that exists, except for God. And such contempt functions like a wall against sin. Secondly, there is a certain hidden sweetness. Thirdly, there is burning desire and languishing love for God. The first ennobles the soul. The second pours the soul into God, so that she will be received all the more deeply into God the more that she tastes of such lusciousness. The third illuminates the soul and makes her shine with light."

Chapter 178. Regarding a Great Sadness because of a Certain Defamation

On the day before the discovery [of the body] of Saint Stephen, a great sadness gripped her because of a certain defamation and false accusation brought against her. And she remained with such a sad and bitter [frame of] mind until the morning of the day of Saint Stephen, and she felt such bitterness in her mouth that it was impossible to remove it even by rinsing with water. And when she heard Masses, she did not receive the usual sweetness, except in two Masses, when her mouth became sweetened during the time of communion, when the priest usually partakes of the Body of Christ.[86] Soon thereafter, the bitterness in [her] mouth, which had been there earlier, returned and that bitterness in her mouth lasted for the whole day.

I believe, however, that that bitterness was miraculous, because the bitterness of the heart corresponded to the bitterness of the mouth. But when it became evening, and that turmoil of the heart had not quieted down, she decided in her heart that she would not want to receive any consolation if the Lord would not console her with Himself. And when she meditated on this, she often intuited the prelude of spiritual consolation, which she always rejected. For she rejected consolation except through the Divine presence.

---

[86] Throughout the medieval period, lay people's access to the Eucharist was severely restricted; some women mystics fought hard for the permission to receive more frequent communion, and a female mystic, Juliana of Mont Cornillon (d. 1258), is celebrated as the champion for the feast day of Corpus Christi. Much of women's paranormal experiences of the Eucharist can be interpreted as compensations for lack of access, as this chapter demonstrates. See Peter Browe's classic survey, *Die Eucharistischen Wunder des Mittelalters* (Breslau: Verlag Müller & Seiffert, 1938).

Chapter 179. How She was Completely Enraptured in God

Finally, she was suddenly swallowed up within into a miraculous light and kindled by Divine fire. And there she was completely enraptured in God, so that she could not be conscious of herself nor anything else except God's infinite sweetness, goodness, and lusciousness, through which she enjoyed and looked upon God. And she became so drunk through God that even if she could have returned to her own being or if she could have had another [kind of] being than what she had here, she did not consider it. And she felt herself so united with God in God that whatever she wished, whatever she desired, whatever she wanted to know, all was present to her. She also said that what she understood there was inexpressible. It is not possible to explain through itself or through any metaphor except for a few exceptions, which are written up below.

Chapter 180. Regarding Patience, What It Merits

In explaining this rapture, she first began with a conversation about patience. Actually, because she had felt uncentered[87] for a little while, patience had been necessary, [and] for this reason perhaps she commended patience as she understood it in the vision. Therefore, she said that patience is of the greatest merit before God, because through patience in any kind of tribulation, a person merits more in a short time than in ten years of activities and devotional practices with all effort and service [expended] for God.

She also said that such humility ought to be very humble, so that when someone suffers something adverse and has patience, he should not think much about merit, as if there would be much merit for him through such patience. Rather, he ought to think and consider that he deserved that adversity, if not then and in that case, then through something else.

Chapter 181. Regarding a Vision of all Human Beings in Twelve Distinct Divisions and their Different Conditions

In this vision, while in God, she saw all the hosts of heaven, angels and saints. She also saw all human beings that live on earth, which are subdivided into twelve divisions and parts.

In the first part, humans appeared as if mutilated, having nothing of a human being except for the face, which was extremely ugly. And

---

87 *in turbatione positae.*

they stretched out as if dead and unmovable. And these are the heathen in whom there is only the image of God, but they are cut off from every virtue and grace.

In the second section were those human beings who had unmutilated human characteristics, but who were black and blind and laid as if dead. And these are the Jews, blind in faith and in the writings of sacred faith.[88]

The third were skinned alive; running to and fro, they splattered those they touched with their blood. These are the heretics, who, running around the world, never stop defiling souls with their errors.

The fourth were the apostates, of whom there are many, who bring many harms to the Church.

The fifth were the thoughtless sinners who without shame and fear sin publicly and attempt to sin as much as they can.

The sixth are the worldly humans, caught in sins but not so publicly. Rather, adorned with a certain respectability of conduct in the eyes of others, they nonetheless engage in fornication, adultery, usury and similar things, while giving alms to the poor, attending church and aspiring to similar good deeds.

The seventh are the hypocrites, who are understood to be all evil religious, all evil prelates, all evil priests. These seven orders are all in the state of damnation if they do not convert.

There exist five other groups who are in good standing.

The first are the well married and those who participate in the *vita activa*, who try to serve God to the best of their abilities and abstain from all mortal sin.

The second are the devout widows and widowers who live a chaste life in the world.

The third are the religious who live under [the vow of] obedience. They enjoy great merit before God, because nothing of what they do obediently is too small to reap a reward, even every step or turn of their feet, [and this] more so [for them] than for others who act or do not act out of their own will, just as it pleases them. Yet in difficult and hard tasks, which they fulfill under the mandate of obedience, they deserve to be conformed [physically] to the Son of God, who

---

88 Agnes repeats and endorses common Christian anti-Judaic stereotypes, as do numerous other Christian women mystics. The common contemporary practice of writing about "women mystics" as if they had no investment in upholding specifically *Christian* claims to supremacy supports, I submit, these anti-Judaic positions. For more anti-Judaic pronouncements in Agnes' *vita*, see chapters 193 and 194.

obeyed the Father and took hardships upon Himself for our sake. And in this they recompense the Son of God and respond to His obedience.

Is there anything else that responds more fully to the Son of God in proportion to His efforts than obedience out of pure love? In contrast, some are deceitfully obedient, namely those who obey prelates, garner their good will and flatter through their obedience. She said that these are similar to maidservants who fawn upon and submit to their ladies in their presence, but steal whatever they can behind their backs. Thus they betray true obedience, which is the most efficacious regarding merit and given to human beings for the purpose of gaining merit through it. And it is of the greatest profit.

The fourth are those human beings who are dedicated to devotion from the heart and to bodily mortification out of love for God. They enjoy great merit, since because of their bodily castigation, they are martyrs, and through their mortification, they triumph over the Enemy and vices as other martyrs have triumphed through their suffering. And because the Church is greatly edified through them, everything is added to their merit through which they edify those around them through their good example. Therefore, like good merchants, they accumulate great treasures of merit.

The fifth are excellent contemplatives, lifted up to God spiritually, united with God through love, endowed with a special friendship with God. They please God so much that their ordinary conversation with God is accepted much like the prayer of a person from among the good ordinary people. They will never be disappointed in their desire if they wish for something from God from [the bottom of] their hearts. In the same way, whenever they pray for God's mercy for someone, it will not happen at the end that the person will be separated from God. In the same way, God finds more pleasure in them than in heaven, because they achieved such perfection while in their fragile body, with the help of grace, and [yet] they still continue in steady effort and eagerness for progress. In the same way all heavenly hosts rejoice over them, because through them, the Lord receives great honor and fame on earth.

Chapter 182. Regarding the Coat of Compassion, which God the Father Gave to the Blessed Virgin

On [the Day of] the Assumption of the Blessed Virgin Mary, when she had taken communion, she soon came into the spirit, and saw the Virgin Mother standing to the right of her Son. The Lord was standing [also], and all the Saints of the celestial court were standing. Also, the Son as well as the Mother appeared well dressed. God the Father gave the Virgin a most beautiful coat, which was decorated with astonishing and pleasing colors. And that coat was very wide and is the garment of compassion, under which the Mother of the Lord hides from God's wrath all who take refuge with her. God, the Father of Mercies, conferred it upon her. And no matter how many this coat enclosed, there nonetheless remained space to receive more. And its capacity for a multitude of those fleeing into its shadow was not diminished.

Also, all the just were covered by the coat not like as from wrath, but they were comforted in grace, and a manifold influx of grace poured into the just because of the merits of the Blessed Virgin. The coat's multi-coloured design, based on different colors, shows through manifold beauty that God offers various gifts and aid to both the just and the sinners through the merits of the Blessed Virgin. Yet this coat was made not from perishable matter, but of a heavenly light of indescribable brightness.

Chapter 183. Regarding the Crown with Four Peaks that the Son Gave to the Mother

The Son crowned her with a crown of ineffable beauty, which delighted the eyes of the onlookers so much that, in contrast to all the beauty of glory except for the vision of God, the joy and pleasure of looking at the Virgin and her crown was enough. For this crown represents and signifies Christ's humanity. It had four peaks. The first peak in the front signified the joy and glory of Christ, which He owed to the Mother's human nature. And in this as if in a mirror, all the saints in the fatherland see and recognize how much love and affection God had and has now for human beings.

The second peak, on the right, expressed the joy and glory of the Virgin Mother, which she owed to her Son's human nature, taken from her into the unity of the Divine person.

The third peak, on the left side, expressed the joy and glory that all saints have through the Blessed Virgin. The fourth or last peak expressed the support of the pilgrims still on the way, whether those living on earth or those existing in purgatory, which is given to them through the merits of the Blessed Virgin Mother. And from this peak, a radiant and exceedingly bright beam was seen reaching down to earth.

This crown did not press down upon her head as if touching her head, but reached up above the head, separated [from it] a little bit such as was also described in the first vision of this little work about the crowns of the saints.

The Holy Spirit honored her as a bride with marvelous affection, so that He works all good things to the honor of the Virgin, which happen to all people on earth at the invocation of the Blessed Virgin, even miracles which are said to be caused by the Blessed Virgin.

Chapter 184. Regarding the Garments, in which all who Belong to God are Clothed

On the first day after the Octave of the Blessed Virgin this virgin came into the spirit after she had taken communion. And behold, next to her stood an image of a most beautiful virgin, completely of the same appearance and form [in which] the Blessed Virgin appeared on the Day of the Assumption, as has already been said in the previous vision. But now appearing without a coat and crown, she said to that virgin, "You have seen me and my coat and my adornments as they are in glory and in the fatherland, [and] have described and explained them. And now also look at the garment in which I appear to you now, in which all ought to dress themselves who will belong to my Son and myself."

Her garment consisted of a tunic of green color, a cape over the tunic in red color, a belt of the color of heaven, which girded her, woven together as if of silk, and completely covered with golden and silver platelets and precious stones. The golden fibula on her chest had four corners. On the upper corner was a red gem, on the lower a very dark jewel, on the right a jewel distinguished by many colors, on the left a gem that shone like the sun.

The green tunic was enclosed all around with an alb, and the sleeves were tight around the arms and closed [at the wrists]. And the Blessed Virgin said, "This tunic signifies chastity. That the sleeves are tight around the arms and closed [at the wrists] so that it is nowhere possible to see naked flesh, and that it is closed everywhere so that even at the tips [of the sleeves] there is no opening, this signifies a double honorability that virgins ought to have, namely in words and customary behavior. Therefore, those who wear open sleeves so that the naked arms can be seen and [those who] wear slit sleeves, are dissolute and brazen in words and behavior. And they do not belong to me.

"The red tunic represents affection for Christ's passion and also for castigating one's own flesh. The belt of a heavenly color signifies celestial desires, which these spiritual garments press upon the soul. The medley of gold and silver and jewels on the belt represents the order of various virtues, so that order can be maintained in all. The golden fibula signifies love. The fibula connects the two parts of the hood, that is its opening, through which the head is clothed. Thus love includes both love of God and of one's neighbor.

"The upper red gem in the fibula signifies patience, the lower very dark one represents dislike and contempt for oneself and all one's deeds, that is a person should never think highly either of himself or of his deeds, but rather always estimate them [and himself] to be deficient. And this is true humility. The colorful gem in the right corner symbolizes manifold compassion and different acts of compassion. The white gem in the left corner symbolizes readiness for good works. And in this manner ought they to dress who belong to me."

Chapter 185. Regarding a Wide Four-Cornered Pillow

Before the [feast day of the] birth of the Blessed Virgin, this virgin became sad and could not be consoled, yet without knowing why she became sad. And she heard a voice within her say to her, "Your soul imitates Holy Mother Church, which is currently in desolation, because she lacks an apostolic head. And those who have to provide for an apostolic head are so corrupted by the heresy of simony that everybody looks out for his own interest during a papal election, intent on putting his own friend at the top. By not searching for the common good, they are thus divided. Therefore, the Lord is so angry that all elements are visibly enraged for the sake of the Lord. And the daily excesses of the air already prove this, by storms and rain showers lasting beyond the usual order of seasons and normal experience and by delaying the fruits of the earth. And this is also indicated by wars and dissensions that rage among human beings throughout almost the whole Church."

And then she wondered whether she herself should perhaps pray for the removal of all this evil. And when she came into the spirit, she saw something like a wide four-cornered pillow distinct with fourfold colors, namely red, white, celestially blue, and blue-gray. And it was said to her that the prelates of the Church, the bishops, the abbots, the priors and others ought to pacify God's ire by establishing alms for pious usage. And this relates most of all to the bishops and is signified by the color of heaven.

Secondly, she was told that one should mortify oneself through fasting, vigils, flagellation, and so on, and those who should do this most of all are those who preside over their orders, together with their subordinates, and the red color symbolizes this. Thirdly, chastity ought to be safeguarded more by the priests, and the color white signifies this. Fourthly, all those poor should be helped, those who were plundered and impoverished because of the wars, and one should have compassion for their misery, and this is symbolized by the color blue-gray.

Chapter 186. Regarding the Prayer of the Mother of the Lord for the People

A little while after this vision, namely on the day of the nativity of the Blessed Virgin, the hand of the Lord came upon her, and she saw in the spirit the Lord and the Blessed Mother of the Lord. And she saw something like all Christian people, everybody in his condition and [social] status simultaneously. And they all stood close together and, pressed together into one [mass], shook in fear as if they expected the Lord to strike them from above, and they did not move or say anything. Then the Blessed Mother of the Lord stepped forward to pray for the people. And the Lord said, "Mother, You intend to pray for these. See now whether anybody moves and steps forward to pray. Now make them pray, and I will reconcile Myself with them." And it seemed to her that some from different groups prepared to pray for the state of the Church.

Chapter 187. Regarding a Very Polished and Shining Mirror[89]

And at another time, the hand of the Lord came upon her. A very polished and shining mirror appeared next to her, in which she saw many great Divine miracles. She related barely an iota of what she had seen, as she said, because it was indescribable. While looking at this mirror, her spirit and soul were filled with ineffable consolation. And she recognized that as the soul is in all parts of the body, [and] makes the body feel and activates the five physical senses in the body, so the soul rapt in God drinks with the spiritual senses, through which she rests in God, [and] is made to feel [everything], and becomes invigorated.

The visual sense of the soul is contemplation, through which she

---

[89] The symbolism of mirrors in medieval literature is vast. For an introduction, see Herbert Grabes, *The Mutable Glass: Mirror Imagery in Titles and Texts of the Middle Ages and English Renaissance* (Cambridge: Cambridge University Press, 1982). See also chapter 190.

sees God and uncertain and hidden matters are shown to her. The soul's sense of hearing is intelligence, through which the soul receives Divine revelations within and understands them without an interpreter. Daniel saw something that he did not understand, but Gabriel explained it to him. He had a vision but not an auditory experience when he saw the hand writing. And when he understood, he had hearing. The mouth or sense of taste of the soul is to taste God's sweetness and to receive His sweetness, and this sense strengthens the soul the most.

The sense of touch is the renewal and transformation of the soul from grace to grace. The sense of smell is desire and lust for God. And this sense grows the most in the spiritual soul and lasts longer than the others do. For the soul does not always look at God, does not always receive Divine revelations, and does not always taste God's sweetness as long as it is in this mortal body, but she can always feel a desire for God. And this is symbolized in Jacob, in whom the sense of smell was more vigorous than the others. Therefore, "Behold, the scent of my son",[90] etc.

In this mirror shone an infinite number of human beings, all of whom she recognized, even those she had not seen before. Some however shone more than others, with a brighter face, and some less so, according to whether they were endowed with more or less virtues. However much all those in the mirror beamed with a pleasing and bright face, nonetheless sometimes something like a little mist clouded some of the faces. And this signified the soul's exasperation over disgust for the deficiencies of those around us. This exasperation is born from the mind's nobility, yet nonetheless, if it lacks the affection of pious compassion, it clouds the eyes of the intellect and hinders Divine contemplation.

Chapter 188. Regarding the Devil and his Mirror[91]

And when this mirror was before her face, a devil with terrifying looks stood behind her back. He had the face of a bull from the forests, horned and black, with burning eyes like fire, and a large beak. And he held another mirror in his hand, placed opposite the first mirror, so that she could see in the first mirror, that is the divine,

---

90 See Genesis 27:27.
91 This image traveled widely in Western Christian iconography. For a recent discussion of some of its cultural meaning, see Kathleen Biddick, *The Shock of Medievalism* (Durham: Duke University Press, 1998), chapter 4.

the devil and his mirror and whatever was in that mirror. The appearance of the devil, however, although horrible in itself, could not cause outright fear in her, and this was because of the exceedingly great joy and Divine comfort and strength that she felt by looking at the Divine mirror.

The Devil's mirror was triangular, and in that Devil's mirror she herself saw the root of her sadness. Her heart often became very heavy with sadness, and mostly because she was unable to serve the Lord as fully as she desired, since the limbs of her body were fatigued. The root of her sadness indeed was excessive physical exhaustion, which she caused through her own fault by applying herself beyond her strength in fasts, vigils, and other physical discipline. From this root is born a sevenfold temptation toward spiritual misconduct, such as impatience, wrath, etc., through which the Devil disquiets even the perfect.

She also said that the armed devil encroached upon a person through a person's excessive physical fatigue. The Devil thus was clad in an armor [made] of tough, black, and rough leather, [and] of soft matted wool hanging down in long [strands], that is, straggly,[92] which signifies excessive physical austerity. The soft wool, however, symbolizes excessive slackening of the obligatory sternness [toward oneself], which stems from immoderation and too much harshness [toward oneself].

She also said that the Devil never ceases to watch spiritual people and encroaches upon them. And since he cannot know all that is in the heart, he watches with an assiduous mind – he has by nature a sharp intelligence – the exterior movement and gestures of people, from which he deduces the interior movements of the mind. And there, he soon tries to seize the occasion by instigating the temptation of anger or pride or sadness, etc.

The Devil also rejoices more over a small temptation or venial sin by a holy person than over a mortal sin of a sinner. Whenever he can unsettle a just person and obstruct him in his service to God, no matter how little, then he jumps [up and down] and dances, because he seems to have diminished and blocked God's glory. And those whom he sees more vigorously engaged in the service to God and more involved in trying to please God, he tries to obstruct more.

---

[92] The scribe injects a Middle High German word here, *zotocht*, to clarify the image.

Chapter 189. Regarding a Human Face Appearing in a Host, and the Savior's Gaze, through which He Pulls Sinners toward Himself

In the year of the Lord 1291, on All Saints' Day, when she wished to take communion and heard Mass, and the priest elevated the Body of the Lord, a human face of miraculous beauty appeared to her. It turned first to the people who stood to the right of the officiating priest, that is to the left of that face, and looked at them for a while. And with one short glance it turned to the priest on the left, that is to the right of the Lord, [and] soon turned its face away from there. She herself however stood to the left of the priest and became frightened, fearing that It perhaps turned [Its] face away from her so suddenly because of resentment. Yet when she had taken communion from that priest, she received the usual consolation. She heard a voice within speak to her, that is she understood, being divinely inspired, that the Lord looked longer to the right of the priest, that is to the left of the Savior, because of sinners, whom He pulls toward Himself with [just] one glance. And therefore it is necessary to look at them frequently. Yet that He looked only briefly [at her], and soon turned [His] face from her, signifies that He pulls the just easily toward Himself. Yet that it seemed as if He had turned [His] face with a certain resentment signifies that God was a little resentful toward that virgin and the friar, the confidant of her secrets, because each one had become indolent in the grace of [Divine] visitation, and lukewarm in desire for the Divine due to carelessness. And for this reason, each one of them accrued another kind of guilt according to Divine judgment: she lapsed into excessive impatience, he, however, descended a little from a state of humility and [got involved] in unnecessary worldly activities, so that he obtained fewer interior consolations.

Chapter 190. Regarding Christ's Injury and the Five Wounds and Forgiveness

At another time, she saw in the spirit a large number of people, who were all in a state of salvation. No heretic, no Jew, nobody in mortal sin was shown to her. And in heaven, our Savior Christ appeared with injuries, and blood flowed copiously from five wounds and was caught in chalices by those surrounding Him. And these chalices [filled] with blood soon seemed to be placed above individual altars among human beings on earth. And when she saw this, she understood most openly, as if she were reading in a codex, that the forgiveness of sinners is given to people on earth through the strength of the

Savior's blood, given in the sacrifice of the altar. And this is a much greater forgiveness than a papal [indulgence].

She also understood that forgiveness exists for two different reasons, through the merit of the passion of the martyrs, and through the merit of the chosen perfect who serve God valiantly in the Church Militant. And among these are some who have never committed a mortal sin; others fell indeed through mortal sin, but recovered perfectly through virtuous penitence.

She saw this also in the following images. A huge heap of honeycomb appeared that seemed to touch the sky. From this heap flowed a honeyed liquid like a river, and from it drank and tasted [it], whoever wished to. This signifies forgiveness that is given through the merit of the perfect saints. And as a honeycomb delights and comforts him who tastes its sweetness, so, from the merit of the saints, sweetness of devotion and spiritual comfort flows into the Church.

Likewise, the same freshly flowing blood appeared copiously, and many who approached [Him], and dipped with their hands in the blood to smear themselves with it, were changed through this to a marvelous beauty. Through this are signified the merits of the martyrs, from which the Church also receives the grace of forgiveness, and the souls devoted to God and the martyrs are beautified.

She also said that those who search for it with too little devotion receive little forgiveness, as well as those who, being wealthy, do not give alms to the poor.

Chapter 191. Regarding the Types of Inflow and Flooding from God into the Saints and Back and Regarding Threefold Love[93]

Lifted up into the spirit, she saw heaven opened and the Lord in majesty and glory and all saints with Him and an inflow and flooding from God into the saints and the flow and flooding back from the saints to God. And looking down, she was shown the world in the form of a sphere, and an infinite number of people were on the earth.

In the fatherland, she recognized a threefold love among the elect. The first type of love is to love God for Himself, and is called the union of lover with God Who is loved. And this love exists in the

---

[93] This is one of Mechthild of Magdeburg's favorite metaphors. For a larger theologico-historical context, see Grete Luers, *Die Sprache der deutschen Mystik des Mittelalters im Werk der Mechthild von Magdeburg* (München: E. Reinhardt, 1926).

elect in the fatherland; and this love is of such value to God that whatever she asks for trustingly, she receives.

The second love is the love of those around us, that is to love God in our neighbor, and to lead him thus to the love of God. And this love is called the attachment of the lover to God who is loved; and this love strongly conjoins God with one's neighbor. The third love is to help another physically for the sake of God. And this love is called treasures and Divine riches, because a person accumulates a great reward with God through these works of compassion. And she saw according to these three types of love something like three beams reaching from God into the elect already in the fatherland and also into those who are still on the way. They receive Divine influences, more or less so as was the case.

Chapter 192. Regarding Christ's Voluntary Generosity

During the night of the Nativity of the Lord, awakening before midnight, she felt a Divine visitation coming upon her earlier while asleep. Marveling over God's goodness, she thought that she had not prepared herself for such great grace. And the voice within spoke to her as if reproaching her, "You poor little one! What do you think, what do you believe – that the Lord visits you because of your prepa-rations? The Lord gives His gifts freely to whom He wishes, when He wishes, and how He wishes." At this, Divine consolation began to increase within her.

Then she prayed in her heart that the Lord would decide to grant her a span of time to pay off the debt of her prayers to God. For as often as she was flooded with Divine consolation, she was unable to do anything but to be completely free for God, and it vexed her when she was forced to drop the scheduled sequence of her prayers for a consolation of the spirit. The Lord therefore fulfilled her desire. When her prayers for that hour were however fulfilled, she began soon to be flooded more intensely with spiritual consolation.

And then the bells sounded for Matins, and she went to the Church of the friars. And there the hand of the Lord came upon her, and rapt within herself in a miraculous light, she saw a very small boy, lying inside her with His head turned toward her right side, and as often as the boy moved, she was filled with an ever new revelation.[94] From

---

[94] Later women mystics developed ecstatic pregnancy into an elaborate spiritual system. See Rosemary Hale, "*Imitatio Mariae*: Motherhood Motifs in Devotional Memoirs", *Mystics Quarterly* 16 (1990): 193–203. For an astute analysis of the gender politics of *imitatio Mariae* in a Franciscan context, see Catherine M.

that hour on, that is from midnight to the late evening the following day, she was kept in those revelations and consolations, so that she neither spoke a word nor partook of any food, except that she swallowed a [raw] egg in the evening. The revelations were of this kind.

Chapters 193 and 194. Regarding the Birth of the Blessed Virgin, How Christ was Born from her, and Regarding Sodomites

In that light, in which she was taken up, appeared the Blessed Virgin before she gave birth, and at the hour of birth. And the Blessed Virgin Herself had a very devout face, full of grace. And while she was bright and shining before the hour of birth, during the hour of birth she appeared [to be] much brighter. She was alone when she gave birth, except that in place of midwives, a multitude of countless angels were all around her and the boy. Some sang praises of God, others looked after the boy and His Mother, and although all the angels shone with a sparkling light, some radiated with such splendor that they dispersed the darkness of night. All the angels worshipped that boy. At the hour of birth, the Blessed [Virgin] was infused with such Divine sweetness beyond her endurance that she could not bear the tenderness of such sweetness. She collapsed and physically fainted, not because of pain, but because of the sweetness of ecstasy. And God intended that the boy would be placed onto the earth after parturition like other boys. This would not have happened if the Blessed Virgin had been in control of her strength.

The manger was large, and the Virgin Mother lay with the boy on straw in the manger, and when Joseph finally joined them and saw the boy, he fell on the earth full length and face down, and worshipped the boy.

And in this revelation, she saw the Magi coming from the Orient and, as she said, on certain horses, which she had never seen [before]. Therefore, it is believed that they were camels. Each of them carried a large, well-filled pack behind the back on the horse [camel]. They also carried with them what food they needed. And a big star preceded them in the air [and] sufficiently close to earth. They traveled wearing crowns, and it took thirteen days from their

---

Mooney, "*Imitatio Christi* or *Imitatio Mariae*? Clare of Assisi and her Interpreters", in Mooney, ed., *Gendered Voices: Medieval Saints and their Interpreters* (Philadelphia: University of Pennsylvania Press, 1999), 52–78. For another example of this swelling, see chapters 195 and 196; for Jesus as mother, see chapters 82 and 115.

home to come to the boy. The first, oldest king was clad in completely white garments, that is a tunic, a throw over the tunic, and a coat. He wrapped himself in the coat in the way apostles are painted. The others were dressed in the same way, except that the second or the one in the middle had bi-colored clothing, that is a mix of the hyacinth color and black, and the last one had red garments.

She also saw about a hundred shepherds, who tended their herds. They were not hirelings, but tended their own herds. Several of them actually went up to Bethlehem for the census, so that they would let themselves be accounted for according to the edict of Augustus Caesar. They took their herds with them, since their money and wealth was in the sheep. And many of them during that night remained in the fields, so that they would evade the commotion of the crowds that gathered in the city. And all those shepherds were devout and God-fearing men. Also, a multitude of angels appeared above them in the air, much like a circle or a crown, and sang, "Glory to God On High",[95] etc.

She also said that all created beings felt the birth of the Savior, except for that being for whom He had become human – he did not feel it. These are to be understood as the unbelieving Jews, who do not acknowledge Him through the testimony of Scripture. Water felt Him, which was turned into the sweetness of oil. Earth felt Him, which became more fruitful where the beam of the star that appeared. Fire acknowledged Him, because it offered light to illuminate that night. Air acknowledged Him, which was sprinkled with a sweet scent in the hour of the nativity. The most wicked people did not tolerate such sweetness, who once perished in Sodom in the stench of sulfur and fire.[96] Such people, I declare, were all extinguished by the sweetness of smell. This was the first Divine miracle during the

---

[95] See Luke 2:14.
[96] On sodomites in Christian theology, see Mark D. Jordan, *The Invention of Sodomy in Christian Theology* (Chicago: University of Chicago Press, 1997). This legend is discussed at some length in Dinshaw, *Getting Medieval*, pp. 85 ff. Dinshaw uses as her primary source the version found in the Augustinian John Mirk's *Festial*, written approximately a hundred years after Blannebekin's *vita* was composed. "As Saint Augustine says: 'When Christ was to be born, the world was so full of darkness of sinful living, and namely of the sin of lechery, and of the sin against nature, that he almost declined to be born of mankind.' Therefore, that night that Christ was born, all those who engaged in the sin against nature died suddenly throughout the world, demonstrating how horrible that sin is before God's eyes." Dinshaw, op. cit., p. 85. Unlike this version, Blannbekin and her scribe group Jews and sodomites into one category.

birth of the Savior, that immediately when Christ was born, those all died, and all lay stretched out on the ground, face down, as if they were trying to hide their faces from the unbearable sweetness.

Chapter 195. Regarding the Little Verse, "My Heart and my Flesh",[97] etc.

It also happened to her during the holy night of the Nativity, when the Lord came to her earlier during sleep with His sweet blessings, as was said above, it happened, I declare, that her whole body swelled up, even the veins. And she felt in her soul such a sweetness of spirit and in all of her flesh not a sexual[98] but a chaste delicious pleasure, that she knew that truly no delight on earth could be compared to those two pleasures, namely those of the soul and the body [mentioned above]. And there was nothing under the sky that could please her in comparison to that joy, with which she was filled in that double sweetness of soul and body. I however was reminded of that little verse, "My heart and my flesh rejoice in the living God."

She felt, however, rather intense pain in the joints of her whole body. And yet, that pain, even though it was intense, was exceeded by the magnitude of the already mentioned delight and consolation. This happened to her every night from the Nativity of the Savior until the Octave of the Epiphany. Late on the last day before the Octave, a certain restlessness and impatience also befell her. And from then on, the swelling and pain, joy and delight did not happen to her again.

Chapter 196. Regarding the Mutual Closeness of this Virgin's Soul and Christ and Regarding Patience

When the swelling[99] came upon her, she soon fell into ecstasy and then received many revelations. For it always seemed to her that she carried the child Jesus within her, as in the night of the Nativity. While in ecstasy, she was filled with so much sweetness and tender love for the Beloved that it seemed as if she embraced Him with her arms. And they spoke within [her] not with voices, but spiritually, mentally, [and] in mutual closeness in the form of a dialogue – she asked questions, and He answered.

He answered mentally as if He were speaking mouth to mouth, and that which He revealed to her, He soon, as often in a spiritual

97   See Psalm 84:2.
98   *libidinosam.*
99   *tumor.*

vision, explained to her figuratively. She also said that the questions that she asked came to her easily and without any difficulty and effort of thought, as if she had read them in a book.

According to her questions, she received answers and revelations, because patience is the virtue that is the most perfect and pleasing to God. She said three things about it: namely that patience carries as fruit many ears of corn and all works that she accomplishes are returned to God pleasantly and with plentiful fruit; and that [of all virtues] patience prevails the most over the Devil and his temptations; and that the Lord gladly visits those who are patient with intimacy and interior consolation.

Chapter 197. Regarding Humility and a Number of Just People and Regarding Priests

Humility is like a wall that surrounds and protects cities, because the virtue of humility guards the other [Divine] gifts and virtues. She was also told that there are some good people who exert themselves for the Lord in physical effort, and they please God much. Nonetheless, if they would focus once in a while on internal devotions, then they would please God more. These people, because they do not expect to be visited within [i.e. in the spirit and soul], neglect to be [spiritually] focused and to taste how sweet the Lord is. The Lord would be willing to give interior consolations to those people, if they would prepare themselves for this. Others, who work too little for the Lord outwardly in the body and are idle, these the Lord often infuses with spiritual consolation, not according to merit, but out of freely given goodness, so that He keeps them thus with Him.

The first [type of persons] pleases the Lord more, and for each of the two categories [of human beings], she was shown several persons in a vision. She also said that the Lord was greatly pleased with priests who officiate devoutly and that they receive an increase of grace during communion of the Body of the Lord and grow in the Lord. And strength as much as fortitude is given to them during the reception of the most holy Eucharist in order to act with strength and to [be able to] suffer. And she said that this is the reason why religious people can do much in God's service, which is impossible for worldly people [who are] physically strong. And it was told her that the whole Church receives great spiritual grace through the celebration of Mass, but some more, some less so, according to their disposition.

Chapter 198. Regarding the Greatest Object of Holiness of the Church, which Is the Mouth of the Priest

And also, while she was thinking, she wondered what the greatest object of holiness was that belonged to the Church and through which she had greater intercession. And the answer was given to her that this would be the mouth of the priest. And the reason was given, because the priest's mouth absolves penitents, the priest's mouth consecrates the holy Eucharist, and the priest's mouth frequently consumes the Body of Christ. Yet those priests who abuse their own mouths with shameless and dishonest words, and all those who do not become priests yet intended it, those displease the Lord the most and bring upon themselves Divine ire.

Chapter 199. Regarding Those who Boast of the Good, and the Lies of Others

She was also told about certain religious, who only guard themselves against mortal sins and who are careless about their status, and devote themselves to pleasures and bad jokes[100] and fruitless words. She was told, I say, that they are only a little better than he about whom was said, "Since you are neither warm nor cold, I will begin to spit you from my mouth."

Also those please God very much who after Mass dedicate themselves for a while to devotions and do not immediately turn to external matters. Those who do the opposite truly displease God.

She also said that those who boast of their good deeds lose much of the merit of their efforts. Those, however, who display with words or deeds the consolations given to them by God much displease God. And the Devil receives the power against these people in order to tempt them.

She was also told about the lies of the religious, that however much it may be in jest and light, it causes the greatest damage to them, and especially the habit of lying. There are three types of damage that are caused by the sin of lying: the first is that it deprives people of the grace of devotion, and the Lord becomes alien to those religious. The second is that as a worm penetrates an ear of corn and empties it out, so does a lie spoil the fruit of his labors in a religious person. The third is that the Devil gains the strength and the power to tempt them.

---

[100] *truphiis.*

Chapter 200. Regarding Demons and Confession

She also saw demons surrounding the good religious in such density and number as there are particles in a beam of sunlight. And yet they do not touch them, but fly close by as if about a yard away, seeing if they could say or do something from which they can take something to tempt them. And when they noted any sign of impatience or pride or another vice among any of them, they soon jump up, hold on to it, and cluster around it like a sphere.

As a stone is thrust from a machine to the wall of a castle, so they one after the other in turn throw [themselves] on him, as if one stone after the other is thrown, in continuous temptation, and this [even] when it was only a small thing he did. Yet as soon as one who is tempted in this way returns to his heart and does penance, that ball of demons dissolves and they fall to the earth like dripping water.

She also said that diligent confession achieves much. As any object thrown into the water swims and flows by and with the water [current] slips away from the eyes of the onlookers, so [does] a sin [escape] the attention of demons through confession.

Chapter 201. Regarding the Light of Truth and Teachings[101]

Before the Feast of Purification of the Blessed Virgin, she took communion, and coming into the spirit, she saw the whole world illuminated by an unfathomable light. And many were as if blind in this light and did not see this light. And it was given to her to understand that this light is the truth of teachings and the teaching of truth, which had already lit up the whole world. The blind, however, who do not see the benefit of the light, are the damned, who do not see the word of teachings. The teachers of the word of God shone like the sun. Some shone with a light [the force] of one sun. Others shone with double [the force of] the light of a sun. Others sparkled with triple [the force] of the light of a sun. The first are teachers of the word and preachers without [good] work[s]. The second are those who teach word and work. The third are those who teach word and work and who desire God with a heart raised through grace and who love ardently.

---

[101] *doctrina.*

Chapter 202. Regarding the Treasure of the Universal Mother Church and Regarding Compassion

On the day of Saint Scholastica, when she had heard Mass, the hand of the Lord came upon her. And she was in a great light and saw the merits and the treasure of the universal Mother Church in such a way that all virtues and virtuous works appeared in separate exceedingly big heaps. Also, good people appeared who added to individual heaps. She spoke thus about compassion, "A shining red pile appeared that signifies the works of compassion of the universal Church." She said that those who renounce everything for God have the greater part of this heap. And she said that this pile is very precious, because a person will gain for himself through works of mercy the partaking in all merits.

For example, when he makes donations to the devout, he merits the reward of the devout; when he gives to those who suffer, he merits the reward of those who are suffering, and so forth.

Chapter 203. Regarding Devout Prayer, Self-Castigation, Humility, Preaching, Charity, Chastity, Love, and Hope

Another heap appeared, large and shining in the color of heaven and signifying devout prayer. And she said that this heap is of greatest merit and value, for the reason that prayer itself causes greater devotion to God in him who prays, and attains more effectively Divine benefits. Also, another shining heap of various colors appeared symbolizing physical castigation, which is brought about through abstinence or any other means of hurting the flesh and violently withdrawing comforts of the flesh, however permissible [they may be]. Another heap appeared, white and shining, which rolled in a circle around the other heaps; it signifies humility, which watches over the other virtues. Also, a flaming heap appeared which grew daily, and signifies the preaching of the word of God. And she said that this heap was most useful to the Church of God. A golden heap appeared, and sparkled like the sun shines upon gold from above. That heap signifies charity. Another heap appeared as if mixed of various colors and flowers, for example roses, lilies, violets and others, which signifies chastity. And many paths opened into that heap. And they signify the manifold assaults and ruses which chastity has to suffer. Every sense of the body has a pathway and exposes chastity to temptation. God however had great pleasure in this heap.

Another heap appeared, larger than the others, of gems and

precious stones woven into purest gold, so that they seemed to be ornaments and precious jewelry, for example, crowns, fibulas, rings and the like, all of gold. The crown represents eternity, which is due to a person through the merit of faith. The fibula represents love, because it links two simultaneously, that is God and a human being, like a fibula [links the] two parts of the opening [front] of a hood. The ring signifies hope, which expects the consummation of the betrothal. The gold, into which the gems were woven, represents God Himself.

Chapter 204. Regarding the Golden Palace Suspended in the Air, and the Two Young Women, That Is Justice and Compassion

In the year of the Lord 1292, on the Day of Perpetua and Felicitas, she came into the spirit during Mass, and saw something like a palace and as if completely made of gold and rather large, raised up and suspended in the air. It was, however, translucent and bright, so that whatever was inside the palace was clearly visible. And she saw in the palace two young women, very beautiful, dressed in shining and translucent gold. And one of them had two blank swords, which she sharpened. When she had them sharpened, the other virgin always tore the sharp swords from her hand and broke them. When those were broken, the first virgin again had two swords, which she sharpened. When those were sharpened, the second virgin again tore them away and broke them. These actions also alternated in turn without cessation, so that one always sharpened two swords, which the other broke, and as often as one woman broke [them], the other again sharpened two.

She also saw many pathways leading up to that palace from all directions, and many diverse people walked along those paths, carrying gifts, which that virgin accepted who had broken the swords. And through this, she was strengthened so that she became more powerful than her companion who sharpened the swords was.

The virgin who sharpened the swords had a serene but serious facial expression, and she is Divine Justice. The other however had a beautiful and enticing face, and she is Divine Compassion. The two sharpened swords are the severity of Divine punishment, that is the real [material] sword of wars and the pestilence of physical death, with which the Lord threatens clerics as well as the laity because of the Church's neglect in the election of the shepherd and pope.

The different pathways and the people walking toward the palace are the different ranks of the good. In admiration of their merits, Divine Compassion breaks [Divine] wrath. Therefore the psalm, "When you will be wrathful, you will remember compassion."[102]

Chapter 205. Regarding Confession

In the year of the Lord 1292, on the first Sunday of Lent, after she had taken communion, she came into the spirit and saw as if all the Christian people. And many of these appeared black like Ethiopians,[103] others were bleary-eyed, others had a veiled face, others had bright eyes and beautiful faces. They went to confession, however, and confessed their sins to secular priests as well as to the religious (i.e. friars). The good confessors, however, were luminous, and their faces shone more brightly than the sun. And she was told, "Those who are black like Ethiopians are the sinners who remain in sin and in the intention to sin. The bleary-eyed and blind are those who are as if swaying to and fro. They have good but weak intentions, as if they would say, 'I would gladly let go of my sins if I could.'

"Those who had as if a veil in front of their faces are those who with the veil of exterior perfection, for example, with frequent confession and other signs of religiosity, cover up interior imperfection and have less religiosity within than without. Nonetheless, they belong to the number of the good. Those, however, who appear with bright eyes and a beautiful face are those who remain always in good and firm intention, not less so after Easter than during Lent. And they always strive to please God. Their conscience is always clear."

Also, when she saw this vision as if in the spirit, in the same way, she also saw everything externally with her eyes, so that some people appeared with a black face, others bleary-eyed, others had a veiled face, others a neat and beautiful face. And she had this vision all throughout Lent. And she often hid her face, because she felt loathing seeing so many deformed faces, knowing that these deformities represented the interior deformity of the soul. Also, she felt pain because of this vision and said in her heart, "O Lord, what does it benefit me to see this?" And the Lord [said] to her, "So that you

---

[102] See Revelations 3:15–17.

[103] Note the negative encoding of blackness; Africans join the abject group of sodomites and Jews; her light mysticism reveals its (geo-) political underpinnings and a preview of racism to come. For other shades of blackness, see the allegory of sinful priests, chapter 123. Blackness as sin is here associated with pitch and human faeces.

recognize in how many [ways] and how much God is burdened, and that you suffer with Him."

Chapter 206. Regarding Impatience and Human Praise, and Spiritual Simony

One day, Christ appeared to her in the spirit, dressed in white garments, and as if with all those in religious orders next to Him on a lovely and spacious field. And He exclaimed with a sonorous voice to those who had before them the harvest of their works, saying, "I implore you, protect your fruit from hail and pestilence and fraudulent reapers, that is from impatience, human praise and spiritual simony, that is, that you do not offer people your prayers and devotions for money." And He said, "Oh, you My faithful workers and the keepers of My fruit, all that is Mine belongs to you. Oh, you My true lovers, you are a light within Me; and as the Father takes delight in Me, so do I take delight in you. Oh, My true lovers, whose love always rushes upwards to gain [ever] greater grace, I am giving Myself to you. Oh, true lovers of your neighbor, by converting him, I share and will share with you Myself and My power. Oh, true lovers of your neighbor, by helping him physically, I install you over My goods and riches."

Chapter 207. Regarding the Annunciation of Jesus Christ

In the year of the Lord 1293, on the Annunciation of the Incarnation of the Lord, the feast of the Blessed Virgin, when she had taken communion, rapt within in the spirit, she saw the heart widen and illuminated by a miraculous light. And she recognized in that light that, as it were, five miracles happened to the Blessed Virgin when she conceived the Son of God, that is:

First, that the Son of God assumed human form from the blood of the Virgin. In this way, the devout soul, receiving with dignity the Holy Eucharist of the Body of the Lord, becomes transformed into the image and similitude of Divine Love.

Second, as the Blessed Virgin became strengthened in grace during the conception of the Son of God, so that she could not sin from then on, so the devout soul, taking communion of the Body of the Lord with dignity, receives greater strength and aversion to sin.

Third, the Blessed Virgin had [felt] great Divine Love while conceiving the Son of God. Likewise, the devout soul, when receiving devoutly the Body of the Lord, is ignited by Divine Love.

Fourth, the Blessed Virgin completely submitted and united her will to the Divine will, so that whatever God willed from then on was also pleasing to her, that is the Virgin's will. Likewise, the devout soul also unites with God through the will in the force of the sacraments and was in harmony with Him.

Fifth, during the conception of the Son of God, several angels were sent for the protection of the Blessed Virgin. Likewise, a devout soul who is taking communion with dignity is helped and protected by several angels because of grace and the veneration of the sacrament. They all say thanks for the fruits of devotion of this very soul by leading her to the Divine countenance.

Likewise, as the Blessed Virgin gave birth to the Son of God, the fruit of our salvation, so the devout soul gives birth to the fruit of good works. And in the way the angels attended to the birth of the Blessed Virgin, so they attend to the birth of the devout soul; they bring before God the fruit, namely that of good works and devotion.

Chapters 208 and 209. Regarding the Prayers of this Virgin, and the Carnal Temptation of this Virgin by the Spirit of Fornication, and the Intense Pain of her Body

All throughout Lent, this virgin used to say five thousand Our Fathers and as many Hail Marys with as many genuflections, falling down on her face, so that she completed the number of those prayers on Easter Day. And then she brought the sacrifice of those prayers to the Savior as a gift of thanks for the act of the Passion of the Lord. And behold, the angelic devil bore this with chagrin. One day, when she engaged in these prayers to thank God for such great benefaction, in memory of the mistreatments and ridicule, the sufferings and tribulations of the Passion of the Savior, that ancient enemy approached, transfigured into an angel of light, and said, "What is it that you do? Who is it that would not be perturbed, if the troubles, which he had once suffered, were thrown into his face? Why then do you throw those mistreatments at Him every day?"

She, however, recognized the devil's deceit, and said, her mind incensed in the fervor of spirit, "Oh, you good-for-nothing scoundrel! Because of this, I will now give thanks more often and fervently to my Redeemer due to His great dignity." And this she did. And soon the devil left, as if hit in the face and troubled, leaving behind the remainder of his evil. Her flesh soon began to be tempted with the spirit of fornication, which she never tolerated. But through God's grace, she quickly escaped such suffering.

Yet when she had brought such a sacrifice of prayer before the

Lord to give thanks through several Lenten seasons, it happened finally, in the year of the Lord 1293, that this virgin went to St. Michael on the day of Easter after the friars' Matins, which she had attended. And there, she attended Matins as well. Kneeling before an altar in the church, she brought before the Lord the completed number of the above mentioned prayers. And in a prayer of supplication, she commended herself and a certain number of her friends joined to her in devotion to the Lord. She desired in her heart and prayed to the Lord that, if the Lord would give a favorable hearing to her regarding this group, for which she herself had prayed, the Lord Himself would give her a specific sign, namely that she also would feel the pain and bitterness which the Lord Himself had endured on the day of Passion.

And soon a voice came to her [speaking], "Quickly move behind the altar." Yet when she came behind the altar, she immediately began to feel the most excruciating pain throughout all of her body in the extremities and the joints of the extremities of her whole flesh, so that she could not hold herself [up] and fell to the earth. And through this she was not less crucified in her heart, but rather the pain and bitterness of the Passion were as great in her flesh as in her heart so that she earnestly believed that she was about to breathe her last breath [lit. exhale the spirit]. And she did not believe that the pain of death could be compared to this anguish. And although her crucifixion was most intense both in body and heart, she was nonetheless not less filled in heart and soul with a miraculous and indescribable sweetness and bathed incessantly in an exceedingly abundant stream of devout tears. And when she thus expected death, and death was not given to her, she then thought of Blessed Clare, how she had lain from the day of Easter to . . . [text missing] as if soulless and immobile. She began to feel anguish that she was not home in a hidden and for her [situation] appropriate space.

The reason was that she could not in any way move herself away from the place where she lay, until she prayed in her heart to the Lord that if she were not to die from such bitterness of anguish, the Lord should give her strength to leave that place and perform her usual prayer exercises. For she was always very careful and diligent to say her hours. And behold the miracle: pulling herself together, she regained her strength, got up, and left, yet the pain did not ever return.

Chapter 210. Regarding an Invocation of the Blood of Christ and a Demon who Pulled her away, etc.

On the Day of the Resurrection, when she had said Matins, she sat down next to the bed with the intent to rest, but was very tempted to go to bed to rest. She resisted, however, and said to herself, "You will not go to bed until the Lord rises first."

For she assumed that it was still before the hour of Resurrection. From Wednesday on until that hour, she had not entered her bed to sleep. And when she so wished to rest while sitting, then a demon appeared who used bodily force against her and pulled or carried her from the place where she sat to the door of her chamber, as if he wished to carry her away. Then she began to invoke the Lord by [His] Resurrection and other incantations so that He would tear her from the enemy. And she heard a voice speak, "Say: Lord Jesus Christ, because of Your love, the boiling blood, that is my hot blood,[104] help me!" And immediately, she broke out in these words with great devotion, speaking, "Lord Jesus Christ, etc." And soon the enemy left because of this incantation, leaving her before the door of the chamber.

Then she said to the Lord impatiently, yet with reverence, "Oh Lord, why is it that after so many of Your vindications with which You have deigned to comfort me so generously these days, You permit the enemy such license against me?" And the inner voice said to her, "This happened with the order that the Lord make it known to you and that you may learn by experience how strong the blood of Christ is and the invocation made for the blood of the Lord Jesus Christ."

Chapter 211. Regarding the Dancing Faith

After some days, it happened that she talked with me about the Catholic faith. And after we took leave from each other, she herself began to think about the faith, since she possessed great devotion and pleasure in the faith of Christ. And on the same day in church, during the Compline of the friars not far from the altar of the Blessed Virgin, the hand of the Lord came over her. And lo, a young girl appeared, with the most beautiful face and a golden crown and something that

---

104   The anonymous scribe inserts another Middle High German term, *min heize bluet*, "my hot blood". Equally violent movements, including that of objects, caused by demons are reported for Agnes's contemporary, the German stigmatic Christina of Stommeln (d. 1312).

seemed to be made of delicate and long silk. And clapping her hands, with a happy countenance she festively danced on the highest step around the altar of the Blessed Virgin.[105] She was also bathed in a boundless light of many colors.

This virgin, however, wondered who this girl might be that danced so happily and moved so proudly. Then the girl told her, "I am your faith. The other virtues pledged themselves to humility; I alone, on the other hand, seized pride and glory for myself, because they belong to me." But she [Agnes] did not understand how pride could belong to her. Then the girl said, "I am proud and praiseworthy above all sects and false teachings which are putrid in the sight of God. I alone enjoy truth and I possess it."

Within a short while, this apparition had consoled, animated and physically strengthened this virgin who had before felt desolate, sad and physically weak.

Chapter 212. Regarding Jurisdiction and the Warrant of a Time for Penitence

At another time, when she came into the spirit, she saw the Lord sitting on a throne of judgment and [with] a golden scepter in His hand, which was very pointed at the end. Also, a large group of religious of different ranks was by His side. And He led an inquiry into the state of Christians. Then all in one voice answered, that all simultaneously fell away and had become rebels against Divine order. Then the Lord said, "What do you advise me to do?"

Then all prostrated themselves on their faces and asked the Lord to show compassion with them and give them a time of penitence. Getting up, the Lord said to them, "I have accepted your pleas and grant them a time for penitence so that they may turn away from their evil ways. I have indeed considered gravely assailing the whole earth, especially the clergy and the secular powers by being overthrown by those below them. However, I will do something so that all will have the opportunity to invoke Me. Likewise, I had considered to afflicting the approved orders and pressing them down with unimportant people."

---

[105] As in the case of Agnes's habit of altar kissing, this, too, represents spatial transgression and usurpation of masculine sacred space.

Chapter 213. Regarding the Holy Spirit and His Ways to a Person

In the year of the Lord 1293 on the day of Pentecost, when she had taken communion, she was suddenly filled with such sweetness of spirit that it spilled into her flesh in such a way that there was not one place on her whole body where she could not feel physically the invaluable sweetness. And she remained in this sweetness physically as much as spiritually for the whole day, flowing over with delights and spiritual joy. Once she was rapt beyond herself, but then she gained a hold of herself, and so she spent that day without doing anything else, neither eating nor drinking nor speaking any word[s].

And when she marveled at the goodness of God because of that great sweetness poured into her soul and spread through her flesh by God, she took a little honey, which she had with her in the house, and placed it on her tongue. And she said that it seemed to her that the honey was bitter in comparison with that sweetness. And she also thought in her heart, "Oh God, if I would know the ways of the Holy Spirit, in which He comes to a person!" Then, taken into the spirit, she understood that in all good deeds, done purely for God, the Holy Spirit comes and dwells. Yet He comes in a special way in honey, oil, water, and fire.

Threefold in honey: first, when the soul is flooded with so much sweetness that it flows into the body, and the flesh feels a certain unheard-of sweetness; secondly, when a prayer tastes good to a person and becomes sweet, the word of God as well as Mass and the like and spiritual devotions. Third, when the soul is rapt in ecstasy because of the tenderness of spiritual sweetness, with the external senses asleep.

Threefold in oil: first, when the soul is calmed through the Holy Spirit's anointing and becomes strong in herself and gentle towards her enemies and neighbors. Second, when the yoke of the Lord becomes sweet to her and she can physically endure more easily the exertions and devotions for the sake of God. Third, when the soul becomes compassionate over the calamities of her neighbor.

Threefold in water: first in the tears of compunction, second in the tears of honest devotion, and third in the tears of heavenly desire and love.

Threefold in fire: first, when the soul sighs and glows in all good works everywhere, second, when the soul becomes inflamed in divine love, and third, when she is divinely illumined through a revelation of the Holy Spirit.

Chapters 214 and 215. Regarding her Negligence and Punishment and the Flame Emanating from the Savior

On the third day of Pentecost, she was barred accidentally from fulfilling her customary devotions. And in the evening, she began sadly to reflect in her mind how unfruitfully she had passed that day, and fell in great despair over it. And suddenly, an immense physical pain pierced through all of her limbs, through which she was comforted to no small degree. She rejoiced over the Divine judgment, as if the Lord had punished her for that negligence, and she said, "You are praised, o Lord, because You do it best by drawing penance from me." And immediately the hand of the Lord came upon her, and she came into the spirit and saw before her from above a large group of people descend who were all dressed with golden garments, with their heads covered as if with golden veils, so that nothing of them appeared naked except for the face. And they had handsome faces, but were grave and serious-minded.

When this group had disappeared, another followed, likewise descending from heaven before her eyes. Those were all clothed in white garments, with a garland of red roses on their heads and a most beautiful face. They happily showed the joy of their minds in their faces. All these disappeared, and a third large group followed.

They all were clad in shiny red garments brighter than the sun. And in the periphery of this group appeared many from the two preceding groups, obviously some in golden dress and others clothed in white. Yet in the middle of that group, our Savior Jesus Christ appeared, most beautiful and lovely to behold and completely naked, His hands raised to about the middle [of the body] and His palms extended in a way similar to a priest standing at the altar. And the open and gaping scars of His wounds shone very brightly and caused the greatest joy for the onlookers.

He Himself also looked so exceedingly beautiful and amiable that His appearance surpassed all beauty.

Also, a golden flame emanated from the periphery and all around the Savior Himself in the manner of pointed rays. And these rays extended out in such a way that some pointed up to heaven, others down to the center of the earth, and others were poured out over human beings above [the surface of] the earth. She, however, did not understand anything about this, until a little ray of the flame penetrated her chest, set her heart inestimably on fire in Divine love and illuminated it. Then she first understood the sight and, when the scope of her mind expanded, she saw all the boundaries of the earthly

orb and countless people, yet nothing but Christians. Also, those rays
of flame pierced human beings, so that one ray penetrated many.
And sometimes, one person [was penetrated] by several rays. Also,
that flame, dispersed in such a way, was poured into human beings
fourfold, that is through the crown of the head, through the mouth,
through the ears, through the chest. And some people received that
flame in all four modes, but some in some ways and not all; others
did not receive them, however [at all].

She also understood that this flame is the grace of the Holy Spirit
or the Holy Spirit [Himself], which proceeds from the Son. The
flame rising up signifies grace, which replenishes all the elect in the
Fatherland. The flame piercing the earth signifies grace which visits
all the elect in purgatory. The flame spread out above the earth
among human beings symbolizes the grace distributed among good
human beings still living on earth. The flame entering through the
crown [of the head] symbolizes the grace that elevates the mind to
that which is above and that sweetens the soul with the sweetness of
Divine comfort. The flame that moves through the ears signifies the
grace of the Holy Spirit poured into a person and comforting the soul
through the words of a sermon. Yet the flame infused through the
mouth symbolizes the grace poured into a person through prayer,
which makes a prayer savory and brings forth devotion. The flame
permeating the chest signifies the grace of the Holy Spirit that
inflames the human heart to the love of God and illuminates the
intellect. She herself indeed did not understand anything that she saw
before she received that flame piercing her chest. Receiving it, the
soul soon knows everything clearly.

She also understood that the Lord did not visit her because of her
merit, since the day before she had performed her religious tasks less
carefully. She also understood that humility and contrition of the
spirit please the Lord greatly and prepare the soul for divine comfort.
She had caused herself much anguish in spirit because of the negligence of the fruitless past day.

Chapter 216. Regarding the Birth of Blessed John the Baptist and his Sojourn in the Desert

When she came into the spirit during the night of Saint John the
Baptist, she saw Blessed John the Baptist as just having been born and
the Blessed Virgin Mary kneeling before Saint Elizabeth and
receiving the boy in her hands instead of a midwife. When she arose
and stood before Saint Elizabeth, the mother of the child, she said,

"Behold, your boy."[106] This virgin (Agnes) also stood next to the Virgin, the Mother of the Lord. And suddenly, this vision disappeared.

And after a little while, when she wished to prepare again for contemplation, she came into the spirit and saw Blessed John the Baptist in the desert, as if already an adult, kneeling with hands joined in prayer. Yet John was of strong body, had dark and shaggy hair, a serious but amiable and handsome face, a thick but not long beard, dressed in [only] one short tunic, [cut] a little below the knees. His sleeves were wide, but short, so that his arms were bare for about the length of a hand's width. The tunic was shaggy and colored as if in dark and red color like a mixture. In like manner, he was wrapped in another garment over the tunic. [His] feet and calves were bare.

Chapter 217. Regarding Trees, in which were Expressed the Merits of Everybody[107]

Precious trees also appeared in the desert, around which Saint John walked, and in which his merits and virtues were symbolized.

Opposite the desert appeared a very spacious field, in which was a multitude of people, also of those whom she personally knew. Each one of them was next to those trees relevant to him, which Blessed John had. The merits of each one were expressed in these trees.

There was a cedar of slim height, which signifies the intense and grave effort (made) for all good exercises of virtue with pure intention. This exalts a person much before the Lord and makes him incorruptible. There was also a palm tree, which signifies chastity. This palm is infertile for a long time and finally, after many days or years, carries sweet fruit. So it is with chastity, which is infertile in the flesh and carries sweet fruit in eternity.

There were roses, which signify the works of piety that are nonetheless not lifted up from the earth. And they indeed symbolize certain good people, who are still occupied with earthly matters, on the basis of which as if from thorns they engage in pious works, much like roses exude a pleasant scent. There were also violets,

---

106 See John 19:26–27.
107 Allegorical trees were a common mystical topos; Agnes's near contemporaries Mechthild of Magdeburg and Hadewijch made ample use of this image, and it was Bernard of Clairvaux who linked the tree image closely to the Song of Songs in medieval mystical exegesis, perhaps harking back to Origen's commentary on the Song of Songs. See also Margot Schmidt, op. cit., 364.

which signify humility with fear [as they grow] close to the earth and with a face turned toward the earth.

Chapter 218. Regarding a Certain Church, in which Blessed John the Evangelist Preached

Also, a church appeared from the region of this vision, which a large group of people visited. And this virgin walked with the others to this church. And when she entered, she saw Blessed John the Evangelist clothed in priestly garments and the chasuble. He stood at the altar with the acolytes, that is the deacon and the sub-deacon, and celebrated Mass. And Mass had reached the stage of the gospel [reading], when this virgin entered the church, and [then] Blessed John preached. Among other things, he taught this, "The friends of God ought to have great faith in the Lord and take pleasure in all Divine works. And if the Lord would cast the whole world into the abyss, whoever is devoted to God should not be turned against God because of this, like the blessed in the fatherland. In the same way, the Lord said to my brothers and me, 'Go into the world, where you will experience maltreatment.'[108]

"But I say to you: Flee the world and interaction with the secular, because interaction with them is an obstacle to grace! Likewise, do not receive Divine grace in vain [without response], and do not be lazy, but become active after you have received grace! The reason: the indolence of good persons, who are in grace, takes much away. The reason: honor is taken from God and joy from the elect in the fatherland through those who neglect received grace, and grace and progress in grace is also taken from them because of their negligence."

Chapter 219. Regarding Different Types of Officiating Priest

One day, this virgin took communion with great fear. For she feared that she took communion much too frequently. And she thought in her heart that if the Lord would not comfort her in the usual manner, then she would not take communion so often. For she went to communion once a week and was accustomed to being infused with miraculous consolation of the spirit. And soon after she had taken communion, her spirit and soul were ignited with a sweetly burning Divine fire, so that her whole body seemed to become aflame.

---

[108] See John 16:33.

And thus filled with immeasurable consolation, she thought about whether she ought to refrain from such frequent communion. And behold, soon she came into ecstasy and [was submerged in] an immense light, and saw many monks who were also priests dressed for the celebration of Mass. And she saw some surrounded by a dark cloud and understood that they were celebrating with a bad conscience. Although they were mired in some ugly sinfulness, they celebrated [Mass] to remove a bad suspicion from the hearts of others. This way, they might not be suspected of a sin. And therefore they sinned more celebrating in this way than when they committed their previous sins.

She saw others inundated with light, and these were those who celebrated [Mass] with a pure conscience and an appropriate disposition and deserved an increase of grace for themselves, and not only for themselves, but also for all who are in the church of God without mortal sin. And also for those priests, who celebrated Mass to cover up their sins, surrounded by a dark cloud, for those, I say, the sacrifice of those good priests was like a shield against the wrath of God, which they [i.e., the good priests] had merited. And so she saw this in a light which suddenly disappeared and as if in a brief passing.

Chapter 220. Regarding Five Types of Human Beings who Partake of the Body of the Lord

After this, she rested within herself; not asleep, she heard a voice as if of someone reading and speaking, "People exist in five different types who partake of the Body of the Lord. The first are those who take communion once a year, fasting and confessing their sins, namely at Easter. And these are members of the Church. There are others who take communion more often because of a certain devout inclination, but they have not prepared themselves for such a great sacrament through exertion and spiritual exercises, for example fasting, prayers, genuflections, and vigils, as would be useful. And those were reprimanded for this.

"There are others who think to themselves, not because of a liking for sufficient devotion, but through the example of others who take communion frequently, 'This person takes communion so often, and I will and can take communion also.' And they do not prepare sufficiently, saying that they can take communion just as often, and not knowing with how much effort and earnestness the others prepared themselves for communion. Those were reprehended like servants or peasants,[109] who offered unripe fruit to their lord.

"Others take communion often with complete fear. And with effort and the disciplining of all their limbs, they prepare according to their strengths, wetting their eyes with tears, listening to the word of God and devotion with their ears, recalling this to their memory to awake devotion. They strive to prepare themselves for such a great sacrament by throwing themselves on their face to the ground with hands and feet and the whole body, invoking Divine compassion with mouth and tongue.

"It ought to happen like this. These are the sons [of God] and they deserved to be consoled miraculously by the Lord in the partaking of the most Holy Body."

And she said that fear was the foremost issue in preparing for such a great sacrament, meaning that however much someone has prepared himself with other exercises, he should nonetheless always proceed with fear.

Chapters 221 and 222. Regarding the Assumption of the Soul and the Body of the Blessed Virgin and the Church's Indulgence and the Group of the Blessed Ordered into Seven Ranks

On the Feast of the Assumption of the Glorious Virgin, this virgin took communion and, coming into the spirit, she saw the soul of the Blessed Virgin assumed in great glory to God the Father, to her very own honor. And with her was a large group of people dressed in white. And she understood that these were those who had never committed a mortal sin and served the Lord with great eagerness. Through their merits, Holy Mother Church has a treasure of indulgences.

Secondly, the Blessed Virgin appeared in the assumption of the body, covered with a red tunic and a coat with immense width, under which all who were to be saved had a refuge.

Her son, Christ the Lord, lifted her up to His right, on a throne of miraculous beauty, receiving her with great adoration, and placing a crown on her head. And with her appeared a group much larger than the first of both sexes. And these are those who were once in mortal sin, but, having mended their ways through harsh penitence, serve the Lord. And all these the Lord adopted for Himself as His sons. And this group is ordered into seven ranks.

---

[109] *coloni*, i.e. "husbandmen".

The first were all virgins who might have at one point been involved in some mortal sins, yet nonetheless kept the virginity of the flesh intact. The second were the outstanding penitents in whom the Lord took great pleasure; and He praised Himself before the whole assembly of the celestial court because of them, saying, "Behold, these were once my enemies, how far away then, how close now!" And the Lord delights so much in them that their sins are not only forgiven, but they give way to glory and ornament, because they have done penitence fervently, and after the mending of their ways, they progressed in the love of God.

The third are the preachers of the word of God. And she saw there a certain religious, her friend, who had the preaching office, but with only little fruit because of the dryness of his language.[110] Nonetheless, he preached gladly and fervently. This virgin understood about him that he should have the reward for his preaching with Blessed Jacob, who converted few in his life through preaching but nonetheless traveled widely preaching the word of God.

The fourth were the good prelates who lead in justice, and these have a great merit before the Lord. The fifth are the devout that dedicate themselves to contemplation and devotion and strive continuously toward God. The sixth are those who suffer in adversity. The seventh are those glowing in every good work and longing for everything good, and however much good they have done, it seems too little to them.

These all simultaneously circled the throne of the Blessed Virgin like a crown and as if dancing a round-dance, well prepared, now advancing, now retreating, so that now these, then those came closer to the Blessed Virgin. Then whenever he, her friend, came close to the Son and His Mother, he spoke to the Lord, saying first, "Oh Lord, You know the heart and that which is hidden. You know that if I could turn all people through word and work to your love, I would gladly do so." Secondly, he said, "Oh Lord, what do You want me to do?" The Lord replied, "Remain as you are. Also, be patient and humble

---

110 Perhaps the anonymous scribe? Certainly the style of the *vita* would match the preaching style described above; the scribe/confessor might have compensated for his unsuccessful preaching by forming a close relationship with Agnes and documenting her life and thought. Rhetorical and mnemonic devices typical of sermon literature can be found throughout the *vita*. And like a good sermon, the *vita* is intended to increase devotion and facilitate conversion. Unlike a sermon, however, the *vita* is meant to appeal not to a public audience, but to an intimate and private group, most likely other Franciscans.

yourself as much as you can. And as often as you press yourself down through patience and humble yourself, so much more merit will you have. And as often as you master yourself through patience, you have as much merit as if you had turned around a soul." Thirdly, he said, "Oh Lord, you know that I would like to have the best [kind of grace], that is, the grace of contemplation and a special love for you." The Lord replied, "You will not be able to reach this part if you do not let go of yourself."

Thirdly, the Holy Spirit received the Blessed Virgin like a bride and an ample crowd expecting to receive gifts as in a royal wedding accompanied her. And these were dressed in half-girded and cheap clothes, and they signified those who were in sin. Yet by conducting some kind of service to the Blessed Virgin, they hoped to receive for themselves Divine grace through her merits.

Chapter 223. Regarding Angels

In the year of the Lord 1292, on the Feast of Saint Michael, when she had taken communion, she was rapt in the spirit into a miraculous light, in which appeared a large sphere, translucent and illuminating everything. In that sphere, it seemed to her to be all the blessed angels and the souls of the just in the fatherland, and the number of angels seemed to be greater than the number of souls. Also, the merits of the just that still lived in the body all appeared in the Lord like a treasure and the likeness of those people.

A certain large and luminous ray descended from that sphere, like a royal road well smoothed out. This street indeed was divided into four different parts, according to the colors gold, white, red, and hyacinth. And this street was of miraculous beauty. On this ray or this street, angels descended to human beings and ascended to God. Yet they walked in four groups as if on a four-lane road according to the partition of the road. Therefore, some were on the golden path, others on the white part, others on the red part, others on the hyacinth path; and the largest group was on the red part.

And this virgin also understood that the angels who descended on the golden path, were sent to the people who were strongest in the burning love for God. Those on the white path were sent to people who suffered adversity for the sake of God and punished themselves in the exertions of penitence. Those on the hyacinth path were sent to contemplative people who dedicated themselves to the contemplation of heaven. They also brought the purity of their conscience and other deeds accomplished with a pure conscience before God's countenance.

This four-lane road did not extend to those who were in mortal sin, but the angels passed by above and beyond them. She also said that the angels, the guardians of sinful people, were above them in the air, like a circle or crown, and surrounded and protected them against the attack of demons.

Chapter 224. Regarding the Sacrament of the Altar

Regarding the Sacrament of the altar, she also understood in what way it is most agreeable to God and how much strength it has and how Divine inflow works within the priests themselves the grace of grace [*sic*], and not only for them, but also for all the faithful of Christ. She also said regarding angels, that those who were sent to human beings were winged with completely white and translucent wings. Some, however, were not sent, but were always in God and stood next to God, and those did not have wings. After this sphere, she saw a horrible place for punishment, from which a very ugly fire erupted.

About herself, she said that she saw this as closely as if it were there present in the soul, and she neither noticed or felt that she was in any way tied to the body. And she also said, because she understood how she was undoubtedly promised that whatever she asked there from the Lord, she would attain, and whatever her soul desired there was fulfilled later. She also said that this rapture and ecstasy happened to her rarely, except on feast days. And when she received communion of the sacred body of the Lord, then she was often enraptured in ecstasy, so that she did not know whether she was in the body or outside the body.[111] But at other times, there was rarely an ordinary day when she did not experience a visitation, aroused by an ecstasy, but nonetheless sensing clearly that she remained in the body. And within herself, in the depth of her expanded mind, she was illuminated, and secrets were disclosed to her.

Chapter 225. Regarding the Seats of the Poor and the Rich and of Diverse Types of Preacher

After the Octave of Blessed Francis, she heard a sermon and it happened there that the hand of the Lord came upon her in a great light, and she saw the poor and the rich enter a place prepared for a feast. The poor, however, sat on a higher and worthier place above the rich. And nobody showed displeasure about this, but it rather pleased

---

[111] See 2 Corinthians 12:1–3.

everybody, because justice required it, which all loved. When this vision disappeared, she came back to herself. And after a short while, having fallen into ecstasy again, she saw again something like a prepared banquet, where there was a large group of preachers. And they were clothed in sumptuous garments, some white, some golden, some red, and some were dressed in all the colors. And some sat at an elevated place, others at a lower place according to the rank of each one. And she saw and recognized how many simple priests of little reputation were preferred to the ceremonious preachers, because they preach the word of God with great fervor and pure intention, although they do not produce much fruit during the sermon.

Then she returned to herself, and this completely during that sermon. And after a little while, she again came into the spirit, and again saw a magnificent banquet prepared, larger than the previous two. And there was a large group of people, who were all clothed alike in a radiant and translucent garment. And the Lord, Who was among them, was also clothed in that garment. And the Lord seated each one according to his rank. And she understood that these were those who for the sake of God voluntarily suffered afflictions and, for a while, endured hardship with the Lord.

Chapter 226. Regarding the Lord's Sermon

Once, falling into ecstasy and rapt into an immense light, she saw the Lord dressed in priestly garments. The chasuble was of purest gold and embellished with miraculous colorfulness. And next to Him sat the religious of any kind of religious vow. And the Lord preached to them, saying, "Those who have completely relinquished all earthly comfort and consolation and only adhere to me, those I will give five things before all others: first, security in regard to my compassion, so that they can securely ask whatever they wish, and I will grant them a favorable hearing. Second, I will make them more useful as reconciliators for my church, that is as those who can make peace[112] between God and sinners. Third, I will give them daily renewal of grace and the consolation of spiritual sweetness. Fourth, they will not have repulsion toward all that is good, and will be fast in fervor and good deed. Fifth, angels and the whole heavenly court will delight in them before all others."

And the Lord called some people from everywhere [every group]

---

[112] Middle High German insert: *suoener.*

and placed them on a higher level than the others. The others all remained on the earth. And those were the ones who were worthy of His five gifts.

Then one of them arose and said, "Lord, but what will You give those who serve You? May they also not completely give up on earthly consolations?" To them the Lord answered, "When the venial [sins] which they attract in such a way are cleansed through fire, then I will receive them." And finally the Lord concluded His sermon kindly and said, "Sons, do not be perturbed and wary because of the harshness of my words, because I will forgive you whenever you will express sorrow from the heart over your mistakes."

Chapters 227 and 228. Regarding a Certain Friar who Loved St. Agnes and the Tear Shed in Love

It happened on the Day of St. Agnes that one good friar, named Erlolf, died, who was famous and known by [his] holiness, [and] who venerated the Blessed Agnes with singular adoration and devotion. For it has been said that he was born on Agnes's Day and on that day entered the order of the Franciscans, and finally went to the Lord on the morning of that Blessed Virgin's feast when the public Mass was begun.

This virgin, who had the revelations recounted above, very much loved that friar in the Lord because of that said friar Erlolf's devotion and holiness. As soon as this virgin heard of the death of this friar, she began to cry bitterly. And throughout the whole day, she tormented herself with pain and tears, and could not restrain herself until the night. And when she wished to rest after such great exhaustion, she felt as if a hand touched her and a voice spoke to her: "My beloved, look back!"

And when she looked back, she saw friar Erlolf with an immensely large group of virgins as if he were leading a ring dance and holding hands. And next to that friar was Blessed Agnes, whom he had loved so much while he still existed in mortal life, that he always dealt with her in his sermons or communal collations. And behind her, she saw countless virgins with friar Erlolf, who were all crowned with golden crowns, but were naked, and he appeared together with them, also naked and crowned. And that nakedness was not only not unchaste or disgusting to the eyes of the onlookers, but filled the heart of that virgin with great happiness, propriety, and joy.

Then the friar said to the virgin, to whom he appeared, "I am friar

'Full of Honor'[113] and now I am not called Erlolf anymore but Erenvol." Then the said virgin inquired whether he had been in any [purgatorial] punishment. The friar said to her, "From that hour, when my soul left the body, I was until the third hour in a certain fire so bright and shiny that, if each of all the stars of the firmament shone like the sun, they would not surpass the brightness of this fire. And this fire was as incandescent as if all fires on earth were gathered into one. And it was as large as the four-cornered garden that is in the cloisters of the friars." And he added, "The friars have helped me vigorously with their Masses and prayers [so] that I could leave the place of punishment. And you, my beloved, with your tears, you have given me coolness against the firebrand. For one tear shed in fervent love brings as much and more remission of punishment as ten years of retribution, as is testified to by Blessed Augustine, who said, 'Oh tear, how great is your power? You conquer the unconquerable, bind the all powerful, you have more efficacy than ten years in purgatory.' "

Then this virgin said, "Where was Blessed Agnes with her companions during the time when you were in [the place of] punishment?" He said to her, "They surrounded the place of punishment and waited for me." Then the virgin said, "How could they endure it that you were tortured so in their presence?" He said to her, "They watched me being punished without being disturbed, because God's justice demanded it. In that fire, like fish move in a lake this way and that, so did I swim and could not get out, because Divine justice held me back. But now I am in company with them and I enjoy the power of a higher rank with those who are powerful." The virgin said to him, "How did this happen, since they are martyrs?" He said to her, "What are you saying? For thirty-seven years, I have endured the martyrdom of living in obedience [to the Franciscan order]: these, however, have completed their martyrdom in one day or a little longer."

Then this virgin posed questions regarding the rank of the order and its merit, namely, what merit would belong to his order, in which he served God. The friar said to her, "All Franciscans are with God in higher dignity and honor, who serve the order and the rule of the Franciscans while alive, especially because of the poverty and obedience of that order." Then she inquired about friar Siegfried Kufer,[114]

---

113 Middle High German: *Erenvol*. See the reference to Christ's nakedness in chapter 215.

114 *Syfrido Coufario.*

who was a companion of the said friar Erlolf during the illness. He said to her, "He will follow me in a short while and make the transition without punishment [of purgatory], if he will only understand his guilt in this – that he pestered his caretakers[115] through impatience. But he will not reach such glory as I did, because he has not toiled in service (for the order) as long as I."

That virgin told me in regard to friar Erlolf that while he was alive, she always received from Blessed Agnes whatever she asked for through him.

Chapter 229. Regarding Two Obstacles among the Orders

Once, coming into the spirit, she saw the Lord Jesus Christ clothed in white garments like those of priests, except for the chasuble. And the Lord Himself stood on a hill, which was surrounded by two ditches. And next to Him on the plain appeared a large group of religious.

The Lord, however, with both hands stretched out, called them and gestured that they should hurry to come to Him. And when they hurried to come [to Him] and arrived at the ditches, they fell into the ditches, some deeply, others less so. And some extricated themselves more easily from the ditches, others, however, with difficulty, and so several could [eventually] cross them.

But she understood that these two ditches signify two obstacles among the religious, which impede unhindered progress toward the Lord, that is slackness and negligence in the service of God and laxness of the tongue. In this, all give offense, but some more, some less. Yet for those who come to Him, the Lord distributes gifts with both hands, that is an increase in grace in them and the grace to edify those around them and security.

Chapter 230. Regarding God's Displeasure in Human Beings

On the Feast of Purification, she took communion for herself, and when she had received the usual consolation of the spirit, she desired after the public Mass of the friars to go and visit the churches in the city because of an indulgence, about which she was always very concerned. Then it happened that she became so tired physically because of the walking that she felt less spiritual consolation than what the Lord gave her abundantly on the day when she had taken communion. Finally returning to the church of the friars, she visited the individual altars to kiss them in the usual manner. Yet she did not

---

115 Or servants [*servitores*].

receive there the sweetness of scent that the Lord always used to give her from those altars on which that day Mass was celebrated, as is written above.

But she felt in place of an exceedingly sweet scent a certain smell or stench of burning, as if the altar had burned. This made her very wretched. Such smell of [something] burning always pierced her nose whenever she kissed the altars, and this lasted from the Feast of Purification until Lent. Then she took communion again and then, visiting the altars again, she kissed them as before and then regained the sweetness lost earlier. She wondered greatly, however, why the Lord had seized the usual sweetness earlier. Then she was told, "As the smell of [something] burning does not delight one's sense of smell, but rather annoys it, so it is unpleasant before the countenance of the Lord regarding spiritual people, when the Lord gives of Himself in spiritual consolation during communion, [and] they then take communion elsewhere and distract themselves. This is what you have done by walking through town and to churches, even if you went for a pious reason, that is for an indulgence."

Chapter 231. [No Title]

Once having come into the spirit in church, she saw a secular priest walk towards the altar.

Chapter 232. [No Title]

In the year of the Lord 1294, at Easter, when the Passion of the Lord was being read, this virgin began to piously bring to mind the Passion and the Lord's very great condescension, and to be piously drawn to the Lord. And she heard a voice within her say to her, "Who wishes to experience spiritual delights with the Lord is in need of three things. The first is that he have a heart free of external worries and activities. The second is that he have a heart raised up to the heights through a desire for the Lord. The third is that he praise the Lord in all His works, so that he has no resentment about anything that the Lord does or decides to let happen."

Chapter 232. Regarding the Strength of the Five Wounds of Christ

After this, the virgin, suddenly taken [up] in the spirit, saw the Lord Jesus Christ in an immeasurable light, wrapped in a white cloth like linen, as in that linen in which He was wrapped by Joseph of

Arimathea. But the Lord stood with a ceremonious and friendly demeanor, and the injuries of His wounds appeared uncovered and fresh. Yet around the Lord were five groups of people in abundant numbers.

The first fell down at the feet of the Savior, and this group of people was larger than the remaining individual persons [together], and although they were of an infinite number, they all had enough space [to lie] together at the feet of the Lord simultaneously. These are the penitents, who deserved there to receive forgiveness for all sins and were strengthened in true penitence. The second group stood by the hand of the Savior, with individual persons receiving gifts from the hand of the Lord, that is an increase in grace. The third group received His blood and water, which were welling from the Savior's side, in the mouth and they were refreshed through it. Those are [the ones] who drink the feeling of love and the tears of devotion in their prayers or meditations. Those of the fourth group all embraced the Lord with their arms and clung to Him always in such a way that they were not pulled away from Him even a little. These are the ones who love the Lord in all His works and are pleased with all of His judgments. Those of the fifth group received the kiss of peace from the Savior's mouth and thus became tranquil. Those are the ones who at times are carried away into ecstasy and are admitted to the kiss of inner contemplation.

Chapter 234. Regarding this Virgin's Debasement

In the year of the Lord 1294, when she partook in the communion of the Body and Blood of the Savior, she was taken into the spirit and divinely filled with great consolation, so that she wondered why the Lord would deign to offer her, someone so unworthy and pitiful, so many and such large consolations. Within herself, she concluded that the Lord would do this because of her humility.

However, she rejected this completely with the opinion that she was not humble in anything, but wretched and completely unworthy. This indeed I have always found in her, that she always debased herself miraculously. And in all Divine gifts with which the Lord generously showered her, she always feared that the Lord perhaps would judge her harshly and punish her, because she might receive His many and great gifts unworthily.

And when she resisted in her soul that answer about [her] humility as is told above, she heard a voice say within her, "Five things come together to true humility. The first is that a person always recognizes the Lord as the sole giver of all that is good, without any presump-tions on his part. The second is that although he has done all the good that he can, he considers himself completely useless having done little or nothing. The third is that he always suspects himself to be lacking in grace and because of this always thirsts and seeks more and more for the grace of God. The fourth is that he is physically humble in all (his activities). The fifth is that he feels compunction more than once over a prideful word or a puffing up of the heart."

Chapter 235. The Love of God is Divided into Five Parts

While at Mass during the Octave of the Feast of Purification, she thought about the Body of Christ with great faith and was burning for that salvific sacrament and was filled with great admiration for such a great [act of gracious] condescension by the Savior. And as if she would rebuke herself in thought, she said, "If I would truly love, with how much love for Him ought I to be filled." And when she spoke this silently to herself, she received within herself such an answer: "The love of God is divided into five parts. First, that someone is aware of sinning for the love of God. Second, that someone takes delight and pleasure in God through love of God. And in this love he is joined to God. Third, that for the love of God, someone labors for the edification of those around him through word and example. And this love responds to the Savior and compensates Him in turn, because out of love He has reconciled him with God the Father through His Passion. Fourth, that without any perturbation, he rests in God with a peaceful heart. And through this, he remains in God and God in him. Fifth, that he burns in desire for God. And in this God crowns that soul in compassion and tender-heartedness, in this indeed by pleasing him with spiritual consolations and in the future, by glorifying him eternally."

In this revelation, many persons were indicated to her by name, of which some had all these different kinds of love, some four, some three, some two. She told me that when she was in this revelation, she physically felt nothing at all on the outside, but within, she was filled with immeasurable delight of the spirit, etc.

The person who wrote this had the name Ermenrich.

In the year of the Lord 1318, minus three years, this virgin Agnes Blannbekin, the daughter of a certain farmer, died on the 10th of May. And she died in Vienna and was under the confession of a certain holy friar of the Franciscan order.

Interpretive Essay
Spatiality and the Sacred in Agnes Blannbekin's
Life and Revelations

In chapter 211 of Blannbekin's *Life and Revelations*, Blannbekin's anonymous confessor reported an astonishing incident. After intense reflection on matters of faith, Agnes told him, she one day received a vision confirming her orthodoxy and good spiritual standing. While enraptured, she saw her own faith dancing around the altar of the Blessed Virgin. Faith appears in the form of a beautiful young woman, dressed in expensive silk, clapping her hands while dancing. She declares that she, Faith, is proud and praiseworthy. The vision's transgression, apart from challenging Church injunctions against dancing, is twofold: for one, a good Christian, especially a woman, ought to beware of pride, be humble and self-deprecating; secondly, she ought to keep a respectful distance from a church altar: its spatial location was taboo to Christian women and lay men alike.

Agnes negotiated the ban on nearing the altar not only in one special vision, but quite matter of factly, in her daily devotions as well. Her *Life and Revelations* tell us that she was in the habit of going around town to kiss church altars after Mass (see, e.g., chapter 40). At least from her confessor's point of view, little could be brought against such devotional extravagance. Agnes's habit was divinely approved through supernaturally granted olfactory phenomena. How much other friars and Church officials acquiesced to such a view, we do not know.

These two transgressions highlight the dangers religious lay women posed to an androcentric medieval Church. Not safely put away behind monastery walls, bold lay women could turn the public spaces of Church and marketplace into a stage for the dramatic display of female religious authority. Although Blannbekin's *vita* contains many intriguing themes worthy of analysis, I will pursue here one aspect in particular: Agnes's very public and thus spatially expressed devotional life. I focus on this issue for several reasons: it foregrounds biographical aspects that are submerged in the writings of other Beguines who emphasize the exploration of theological and literary topics more than devotional practices. Secondly, it highlights the centrality of personal acts of devotion for Beguines.[1] Given medieval people's high illiteracy rates, it is important to bear in mind that devotional practice more than literary activity created a local female religious sub-culture. Agnes's accounts are perhaps far more representative of the larger community of religious women than the writings by the few elite female writers whose works have survived and, unlike Agnes's *vita*, are widely circulated today. Through public and private ritual action, women thus shifted the androcentric drama of Church ritual practice and teachings back to female actors. Men had only limited access to their experiential worlds; rigidly defined gender roles more often than not foreclosed male ecstatic and visionary explorations of the sacred. No doubt ecclesiastical male elites had in the long run more political and social staying power. Nonetheless, mystically gifted women could exercise spiritual authority and independence in their respective local communities.[2] Certainly a priest was necessary and desired in administering pastoral care and the rites of the Church to the faithful, but the community expected holy women as well to mend the fabric of affection and kinship ties torn by illness, misdemeanors, and death. Holy women's practices, and even their few writings, surprisingly often found support among priests and confessors, at least on a local level. Agnes Blannbekin's *vita* demonstrates how such relationships were played out on the stage of daily life, both inside and outside male sanctuaries. In her case, her confessor could at the most be a scribe, an observer, an often gentle, but, it seems, on the whole hardly ever a domineering presence. As their many recorded conversations demonstrate, it was Blannbekin who took the lead in applying Christian teachings to local events and community needs. Her many visions on Eucharistic themes even reshaped the gendered meaning of men's celebration of Mass, because it was through Agnes's visionary powers and sharply critical commentaries that Divine presence and the worthiness of priests could be experientially ascertained

---

[1]   See Penny Galloway, "Neither Miraculous nor Astonishing: The Devotional Practice of Beguine Communities in French Flanders", in *New Trends in Feminine Spirituality: The Holy Women of Liege and their Impact*, edited by Juliette Dor, Lesley Johnson, and Jocelyn Wogan-Browne (Turnhour, Belg.: Brepols, 1999), 107–29.

[2]   For a discussion of this issue in regard to the late medieval Beguine Maria van Hout, see Ulrike Wiethaus, " 'For this I Ask You, Punish Me': Norms of Spiritual Orthopraxis in the Work of Maria van Hout (d. 1547)", *Ons Geestelijk Erf* 68:3 (1994): 253–70.

and thus validated (for example, see chapter 72 for Agnes's interventions). Any impact made by her confessor's dogmatic pronouncements must have paled (though not disappeared) next to her colorful and dramatic mystical theatre.

Maps of the Holy

Medieval individual religious lives, both female and male, can hardly be imagined apart from their communal settings, whether secular or sacred. Since its introduction to Europe, Christianity superimposed maps of the holy and unholy upon cities and the countryside alike, creating a religious ecology of "landscapes of worship" and "landscapes of death".[3] Eventually, the concept of Holy Christendom combined geographical reality with ideological construct to the point that both became indistinguishable from one another. Nonetheless, women and men experienced such a geography of faith in gender-specific terms. Somewhat polemically, one might even say that in terms of sacred geographies, a veritable turf war evolved around the most sacred fetish of medieval Christianity, the Eucharist, framed by its location and accessibility in church. Barred from priesthood and therefore immediate access to the Holy of Holies, religious women creatively reinserted themselves as actors into ritual space through ecstatic and visionary physical participation, and imaginatively through their writings. In Agnes's case, women claim eucharistic presence through spatial transgressions (e.g. Agnes kissing the altar and engaging celebrants in different churches rather than staying with her confessor only). Other practices of delegitimizing masculine prerogative are Agnes's visionary preoccupations with male nudity and the priests' less physical qualifications, including their frequent shortcomings, thus questioning the efficacy of the male-staged ritual from its very heart. Perhaps some priests felt that Agnes came dangerously close to "priest-bashing" in some cases. And what could be more anti-climactic than to remind priests that the altars mystically smelled like sweet rolls, the products of female domestic labor?

As I will briefly sketch below, some female mystics also opted for

---

[3] For a definition and exploration of these concepts, see Chris C. Park, *Sacred Worlds: An Introduction to Geography and Religion* (London and New York: Routledge, 1994). For a feminist study of the architectural layout of medieval female monasteries, see Roberta Gilchrist, *Gender and Material Culture: The Archeology of Religious Women* (London and New York: Routledge, 1994).

simply shifting the locus of Divine presence from the Eucharist to
landscapes where women could move more freely than in ecclesiastically controlled sacred space which relegated them to the margins.
Perhaps not least because of their tightly regulated access to male
space, medieval religious women writers have excelled in the
creation of a fabulous imaginary world populated by women. It is in
heaven that Christian women receive privilege of place, it is in
heaven where they see themselves as freely moving subjects and key
players *in propria persona*.[4] And whereas the most likely candidates
for a religious career, that is unmarried women and widows, were
doubly marginalized in secular spaces, lay-women visionaries sometimes even reversed the secular preference for marriage by granting
unmarried women and widows primacy over wives in heaven. Agnes'
confessor, for example, recorded a widow's vision of a beautiful
place exclusively reserved for widows (chapter 139).[5]

Apart from such visions of heaven, we find two main spatial metaphors in Beguine spirituality that de-emphasize the importance of a
church as sacred space. Some female authors elaborated on the aris-
tocratic court with its gardens, women's chambers, kitchens, and
bedrooms refurbished as sacred spaces; other women preferred the
medieval town with its markets, streets, Jewish quarters, shops, and
interior domestic spaces. Each spatial paradigm, apart from the
freedom of mobility it grants, also denotes social standing: the court
is associated with the land-owning nobility, the streets with the class
of artisans, merchants, and peasants.

If Barbara Newman is correct in labeling the writings of the
Beguines Mechthild of Magdeburg (d. 1282 or 1292), Hadewijch (fl.
first half of the thirteenth century), and Marguerite Porete (d. 1310)
"courtly mysticism", and I believe that her term is chosen
felicitously, then Blannbekin's religiosity exemplifies, no doubt,
women's "street mysticism".[6] Of these four authors, we only know

---

4   Agnes calls heaven perhaps not accidentally her fatherland, and life on earth her
exile. No doubt this is a well-worn medieval trope, but it takes on poignant
meaning for religious women in a patriarchal Church. The widow described in
chapter 139 yearns to join other widows in their own special heaven, but is denied
entry.

5   For a discussion of the theological context for female visionaries' concepts of
heaven, see Caroline Walker Bynum, *The Resurrection of the Body in Western
Christendom, 200–1336* (New York: Columbia University Press, 1995), part
three.

6   Barbara Newman, *From Virile Woman to WomanChrist: Studies in Medieval
Religion and Literature* (Philadelphia: University of Pennsylvania Press, 1995).

Blannbekin's social background for certain, since it is explicitly mentioned in the *vita* that her parents were farmers. Given the other Beguine authors' intimate knowledge of the court and their greatly developed literary skills, it is likely that they were well-educated members of the social elites. It is telling that although Agnes was introduced to St. Bernard of Clairvaux's teachings on courtly love mysticism (see, e.g., chapter 130), she deftly rejected his model in favor of the more common role of women as heads of households (chapter 118). Other references to courtly life in Blannbekin's *vita* are extremely rare and even hostile as in the story of her unnamed Beguine companion's sojourn at court (chapters 143 and 144).

A recent study by Jane Chance of the Beguine Marguerite Porete (d. 1310), the religious lay-woman Margery Kempe (d. ca. 1438), and the professional lay author Christine de Pizan suggests that through their writings, the authors "feminiz(ed) male spaces in terms domestic, quotidian, beguine, or monastic, and therefore (engaged in) secularizing the sacred".[7] Significantly, all three writers were women who led non-cloistered lives in or near urban environments. The Beguine Marguerite Porete most likely lived and taught in Valenciennes, the secular writer Christine de Pizan in Paris, and the lay-woman Margery Kempe in Lynn, her career as author stimulated by numerous trips in England and abroad. Kempe and de Pizan left us poignant stories of their physical forays into masculine spaces, whether petitioning lawyers in the courts of justice and waiting for many days in their hallways to gain a hearing or being brought before a bishop for an interview. In all of their gendered acts of spatial mobility, geographic spaces served as markers, maps, and carriers of meaning.

The Court as Sacred Space

To highlight Blannbekin's distinct contribution to our understanding of medieval religious women's subcultures, I will begin with a brief description of the better-known spatial paradigm in Beguine spirituality, courtly mysticism. It is usually associated with the literary productions of Mechthild of Magdeburg, Hadewijch, and Marguerite

---

[7] Jane Chance, "Speaking *in propria persona*. Authorizing the Subject as a Political Act in Late Medieval Feminine Spirituality", in *New Trends in Feminine Spirituality*, edited by Juliette Dor et al., 265–69, quotation p. 268.

Porete.[8] Sociologically speaking, courtly love mysticism exemplifies some of the key aspirations of the nobility. Among these are the right to preferential treatment and respect, freedom of movement in all places and at all times, full membership among the privileged, refined manners, expensive personal property such as sumptuous clothing, jewelry, and books, and fine foods and entertainment as expressions of status.

The paradigm of courtly love in itself is an expression of noble status and birth-right, since peasants were deemed too coarse and brutish to play by its stylized rules. Its basic plot line can be quickly summarized, although it found remarkably complex treatment among medieval spiritual authors, whether female or male.[9] For Christian mystics, the secular courtly love model became fused with elements of the Song of Songs: a "noble" soul, visualized as a young bride, is to be wedded to the "king" at the heavenly "court". Mechthild of Magdeburg writes about this union with delight, but clearly separates it from the devotional praxis of other (lower class?) holy women.

> Then He (Christ) pulls her further to a secret place. There she
> is not permitted to plead for anybody nor to ask questions,
> since He wishes to play with her alone a game that the body
> does not understand, nor the peasants at the plough, nor the
> knights at the tournament nor His loving Mother Mary – with
> all this she cannot occupy herself at that place.[10]

The bride-soul's yearning, her adventures, her courtship, and her

---

8   See most recently, Bernard McGinn, *The Flowering of Mysticism: Men and Women in the New Mysticism (1200–1350)* (New York: Crossroad, 1998), chapter 5, "Three Great Beguine Mystics", 199–266.

9   Among male authors, St. Bernard of Clairvaux (d. 1153) deserves first place, not just because of the high quality of his spiritual writings, but also because he is generally regarded as the creator of courtly love or bridal mysticism. See Bernard of Clairvaux, *Sermones super cantica canticorum. Sancti Bernardi opera*, edited by Jean Leclerq, Henri Rochais, and Charles Talbot (Rome: Editiones Cistercienses, 1957–77). For an analysis of Bernard's appropriation of the courtly paradigm, see Ulrike Wiethaus, "Christian Piety and the Legacy of Medieval Masculinity", in *Redeeming Men: Essays on Men, Masculinities, and Religion*, edited by Stephen B. Boyd, W. Merle Longwood, and Mark Muesse (Philadelphia: Westminster/John Knox, 1996), 48–62.

10   "so zuhet er si furbas an ein heimliche stat. Da mus si fur nieman bitten noch fragen, wa er wil alleine mit ir spilen ein spil, das der lichame nut weis noch die dorper bi dem phluge noch die ritter in dem turnei noch sin minnenklichu muter Maria, mag si nut gepflegen da." Mechthild of Magdeburg, *Das fliessende Licht der Gottheit* (München and Zürich: Artemis Verlag, 1990), I:2, 6–10.

union with the bridegroom form the basis for psychological and theological explorations and are often expressed in a supremely poetic and literary manner. Coming into its own during the thirteenth century, courtly love mysticism developed at a historical moment when the social structure based on a land-owning noble class and its contract with a larger peasant population began to give way to a more centralized, trade- and city-oriented economy. This economic shift also necessitated the rise of a new class of bureaucrats, merchants, and burghers. Culturally speaking, the concept of courtly love mysticism was therefore already in the medieval era in some way nostalgic and sentimental. For one thing, it idealized a medieval social reality that was never quite as idyllic as it became imagined in the writings of medieval mystics, especially in its calculating marriage policies, constant threat of warfare, rule of primogeniture, and enforcement of gender inequalities. Secondly, it abstracted from the economic realities that allowed the luxurious lifestyles of a few through the exploitation of many.[11]

Despite its lack of realism, however, the achievement of medieval mystical maps of a heavenly court for women lies in the fact that the figure of the noble bride afforded women writers a voice of dignity and impressive religious autonomy. No matter how restricted women's actual position in medieval society and the Church was, the heavenly court could signify a heterosexual sacred utopia in which powerful men respected and honored women, frozen in the liminal and transitional role of bride – not child, not yet wife, not yet mother.

The courtly model thus reflected both inclusion and exclusion – insofar as all human beings had a female noble soul, all could claim at least spiritually the dignity that it bestowed. In so far as the soul was conceptualized as noble and Christian, however, it implicitly invalidated the actual status of those who were not born noble or Christian. Nobility for all in the spiritual realm did not translate into a vision of equality in the social and economic realm. Finally, in so far as courtly love mysticism was a romance defined in heterosexual terms, it excluded persons of non-normative sexual orientation. Thus it should come as no surprise that the writings about courtly love

---

[11] For a model of reading medieval religious paradigms from a sociohistorical perspective, see James C. Russell, *The Germanization of Early Medieval Christianity: A Sociohistorical Approach to Religious Transformation* (New York and Oxford: Oxford University Press, 1994).

mysticism contain anti-Judaic theological statements, denigrate peasants and servants, and, to a lesser degree, condemn homosexuality.[12]

The City as Sacred Space

Another type of female spirituality developed contemporaneously with this exclusionary spiritual model of courtly love. It is less literary and literally more commonplace than courtly love mysticism, yet often just as strongly charismatic. I have termed it "street mysticism", an expression of female spirituality that takes as its sacred *locus* not the enclosed court with its romantic intrigues, tournaments, minstrels, walled gardens, and female living quarters, but the open spaces of markets, churches, shrines dedicated to the saints, shops, apothecaries, roads, and hospitals.[13] Yet although socially more dynamic than a courtly environment, medieval towns were still sites that marked boundaries between "same" and "other". For example, not only Jews but also prostitutes had to publicly wear special markers and clothing that made them easily recognizable. Social roles allowed for little behavioral flexibility, and it sometimes took the efforts of an outsider even to recognize a holy woman as holy rather than mentally unstable.

The life story of Christina Mirabilis (d. 1224) reveals the ambiguity that a poor woman's public ritual behavior sometimes could evoke. Orphaned at an early age and living without a male head of the household, Christina and her two sisters subsisted at the margins of respectable town life outside Liege in the Low Countries. After a dramatic near-death experience and concomitant visions of the afterlife, Christina displayed erratic behavior that was cruelly punished by the town folk, thus intensifying her and her sisters' social isolation. Her biographer accurately described her liminal status and the vulnerability it brought. His account makes it difficult to decide what came first, Christina's persecution as a marginal young female, to which she responded with unusual behavior, or her behavior, which triggered cruel retribution by the townspeople.

[12] See Ulrike Wiethaus, *Trace of the Other: Interpretations of Diversity in Medieval Christian Mysticism* (forthcoming).

[13] Medieval authors were quite aware of the Beguines' unusual freedom to roam public spaces without male supervision, and ridiculed them as "loose women". See Anke Passenier, " 'Women on the Loose': Stereotypes of Women in the Stories of Medieval Beguines", in *Female Stereotypes in Religious Traditions*, edited by Ria Kloppenborg and Wouter J. Hanegraaff (Leiden: Brill, 1995), 61–88.

Christina ran from the presence of men with wondrous horror and fled into the deserts [uncultivated areas surrounding the town] and into trees and perched on the peaks of turrets or steeples and on other lofty places. The people thought she was possessed by demons and finally, with great effort, managed to capture her and bind her with iron chains. Thus bound, she suffered many pains and great privation.[14]

It is only after the kind hospitality of Cistercian nuns, and the local count took a fancy to her, that the town's larger community stopped defining her as a demoniac.[15] Christina became gradually socially reintegrated as a holy woman who could be of valuable service to her community, especially through the foretelling of future events and visions of the fate of the dead. Her previous social marginalization subsequently became refashioned as sign of divine guidance, and after much suffering, Christina finally found a safe and socially productive place in her community. In the words of her biographer,

She had insight into many things with the spirit of prophecy and forewarned many to salvation and privately reprimanded many of their secret sins and recalled them to penance. When that unfortunate meeting at Stepes occurred in October 1213 between the duke of Brabant and his enemies where so many hundreds of men were killed, on that very day this blessed woman cried out as if in childbirth and said, "Alas! Alas! I see the air full of swords and blood! Hurry, sisters, hurry! Pray to the Lord! Shed tears lest from His wrath He repress His mercy!" And she said to a nun at the monastery of St. Catherine's in St. Trond, "Run, daughter, quickly run to prayer! Beg the Lord for your father because he is in great danger!"[16]

---

14 "Cum Christina hominum praesentias miro horrore fugeret in desertis, in arboribus, in summitatibus turrium vel templorum vel quarumlibet rerum sublimium, putantes eam plenam deamonibus, tandem cum magno labore captam vinculis eam ferris manciparunt: ubi dum multas peonas pateretur . . ." *The Life of Christina the Astonishing*, Latin text with facing English translation, translated with introduction and notes by Margot King with assistance from David Wiljer (Toronto: Peregrina Publishing, 2nd edition 1999), chapter 9.

15 On this issue, see Barbara Newman, "Devout Women and Demoniacs in the World of Thomas of Cantimpré", in *New Trends in Feminine Spirituality*, 35–61.

16 "Spiritu prophetiae in multis claruit, multos praemonuit ad salutem, multos de secretis et occultis sceleribus in occulto redarguit, et ad peonitentiam revocavit. Quando illa miserabilis congression facta est anno Domini MCCXIII mense Octobri inter duecem Brabantiae et ejus adversarios, ubi in loco, qui dicitur Steps tot centena hominum occisa sunt, ipsa Beata mulier eadem die clamabat quasi

Although I treat street mysticism and courtly mysticism somewhat artificially as separate systems to highlight their differences, we find examples of women and men who borrowed elements from both paradigms. In actuality, both systems fed into each other, especially so in the writings of the Beguines, but also among some cloistered women. The German Dominican nun Margarete Ebner (ca. 1291–1351), for example, although cloistered and of patrician background, offered pastoral work much like a street mystic and drew repeatedly from the paradigm of courtly love in her devotional writings.[17] In her later years, even Mechthild of Magdeburg denounced a bridal mystical model and exclaimed that since she had lost her youthful beauty, she was now better suited to be the female head of the household, with God by her side as the pater familias. As her writing matured, more and more images from ordinary town life in Magdeburg seeped into her writing, but also more descriptions of actual relationships among people.

Agnes, like Christina Mirabilis, Mechthild of Magdeburg, or the indefatigable pilgrim Margery Kempe, left us glimpses of a model of medieval female sanctity that is marked by neither monastic enclosure nor the manners of the court. Her text abounds with references to the concerns of the city commune, to women's presence in public urban space, and their observations of and contributions to the daily vagaries of town life. Blannbekin's notion of Christian piety, though steeped in Christian symbolism and scriptural and theological knowledge, is ultimately legitimized by an array of urban themes and experiences. Blannbekin is shown roaming the streets with her female companions, crossing public spaces, visiting churches and leaving for out-of-town errands. Daily activities become an occasion for reflection and pious interpretation, such as the regular practice of blood letting (chapter 78) or using the lavatory (chapters 90 and 91), the presence of night guards in medieval streets (chapter 127), preparing food in the kitchen, and the necessity of frequenting the market and the apothecary (chapters 26–29).[18] Graphic images illustrate Agnes's alertness to the humdrum

---

parturiens atque dicebat: Heu, heu! Video aerem gladiis et sanguine plenum. Currite sorores, currite; rogate Dominum; lachrymas fundite, ne contineat in ira misericordias suas. Et cuidam moniali in ipso monasterio S. Katerinae prope oppidum S. Trudonis dixit: Curre, filia, curre ad orationem velociter; et roga Dominum pro patre tuo, quia in maximo nunc discrimine constitutus est." Op. cit., chapter 29.

[17] See Leonard P. Hindsley and Margot Schmidt. "Introduction", in *Margaret Ebner: Major Works*, translated by Leonard P. Hindsley (New York: Paulist Press, 1993), 9–81.

[18] Renate Blumenfeld-Kosinski has shown how such attention to daily life was

of daily life, such as when she described cleaning her teeth with a knife and pulling out two flies (chapter 79), unimaginable in a courtly scenario. Her piety is rich in images of strong religious women engaging in secular activity, including the vision of her own faith as a young woman dancing around the altar (chapter 211). Women even usurp masculine activity as in the case of the allegory of justice brandishing two swords, an image which also functioned perhaps as a mystical interpretation of the story of martyrs Perpetua and Felicitas (chapter 204).

* * *

Like her more educated fellow Beguines, Agnes commented frequently and not without prejudice on the status of desirable insiders and mistrusted outsiders such as Jews, Ethiopians, homosexual persons, and visitors from other towns. Ironically, however, the new orders of mendicant friars (Dominicans and Franciscans) frequently began their sojourn in a particular town by living outside the city walls themselves, thus unsettling established geographies of center/margin social identities. Street mysticism, like courtly mysticism, includes the sinister side of medieval Christianity. Yet it also offers a more realistic view of medieval town life. We learn how people were trampled to death when a bishop visited Vienna on Maundy Thursday (chapter 75) or how a priest raped a young woman (chapter 41). In all these events, heaven is still close to earth, as her thoughts on angels, St. Francis, and the future rewards for the poor demonstrate. Earth is a good and sacred place to be (chapter 1), despite all suffering. If God thinks this earth appropriate to provide the stuff of which His Body is made, then in turn no part of God's Body is insignificant enough to serve as an object of reverence. And so Agnes received a vision of swallowing Christ's foreskin (chapter 37). The fact that to Blannbekin it tasted and felt like the skin of an ordinary boiled egg is perhaps the most outrageous provocation to the refined paradigm of courtly love.

What we thus find in Blannbekin's accounts is not so much a

---

quickly satirized by male writers. She quotes French poet Rutebeuf, for example, who declared that a Beguine's "speech is prophecy; if she laughs she's a good companion; if she cries it's devotion; if she sleeps she's ravished; if she dreams, she has a vision; if she lies do not ever believe her". Blumenfeld-Kosinski, "Satirical Views of the Beguines in Northern French Literature", in *New Trends in Feminine Spirituality*, 237–49, quotation p. 241.

female secularization of the sacred, but an innovative transformation of the secular into sacred space to counterbalance sacred spaces created and maintained by male privilege. This, however, is only possible because Agnes is skilled in the production and analysis of her ecstatic and visionary trances as well as of other types of super-natural perception. Perhaps, the gentle rain that settled the dust in the streets during a visit by the Bishop of Passau appeared to ordinary believers only as a welcome respite. For Agnes, it was clearly a Divine sign affirming her special status before God (chapter 75). Blannbekin's mystical perceptions carried conviction for both her and her male confessor, who could, however, only enter her spiritual world as passive bystander.

Women's Ritual Action and Writing as Sacred Performance

The biographical momentum of sacralizing secular space is repeated in Agnes's ritual efforts to sacralize the secular flow of time: Blannbekin's *vita* is one of the earliest examples of a spiritual diary. Its structure is determined most of all by the liturgical year, which more than any other temporal markers (such as the seasons) in Agnes's life frames her self-understanding and social role as a Beguine.[19] Yet whereas her priest confessor relied on well-established routines of his liturgical and pastoral duties, Blannbekin, like other lay religious women excluded from the priesthood, responded to androcentric marginalization with the invention of gynocentric rituals of devotion. Street mysticism thus worked with images of public life to which most people and especially women had easy access. To be sure, this included an affirmation of sacred symbols used during collectively shared religious rituals, such as the Eucharist, relics, or the elevated role of the priest during Mass. Yet street mysticism also sanctified daily life, especially transactions and events that would ensure or jeopardize personal and communal well-being: child care, illness and death; abnormal occurrences that could be read as omens, whether of animals, people, or the weather; military events; and even quotidian actions such as cooking, main-taining a household, and using medicines. Both Mechthild of Magdeburg and Agnes Blannbekin mention pastoral activities that include care for the dying and the dead through prayers, funeral atten-dance, and communication with the dead. Note that Christina

---

[19]   On the importance of the liturgy for Beguines' spiritual life, see Penny Galloway, op. cit.

Mirabilis, for example, told a nun about her father who was in danger: it was expected not only that she would know something about his well-being, but that she would also be knowledgeable about family networks.

Specially gifted holy women were also recognized as healers of the living. As in the case of St. Elisabeth of Thuringia (1207–31), one of the earliest models of urban female sanctity, and like Agnes associated with the Franciscan order, even a holy woman's corpse was seen as charged with the ability to heal.[20] Marie d'Oignies (1177–1213), celebrated as the first ecclesiastically recognized Beguine by her male biographers, helped women in difficult childbirth even after her death: parts of her clothing were wrapped around the woman in labor.[21] The belief in a saint's curative powers has in numerous cases persisted until the present, as on-going local and even transregional cults of their relics and gravesites demonstrate.

In these informal communal networks, street mystics such as Agnes Blannbekin, Marie d'Oignies, or Christina Mirabilis were remembered through their ritual performances and active ministry to an urban population that included secular and religious groups. Courtly mystics, on the other hand, tended to leave their mark as authors and teachers of groups of spiritual seekers, often as especially well-educated and articulate supporters of the new orders. The metaphor of the noble court thus may also have functioned as a code for unusually high theological and scriptural knowledge as well as for a more exclusive sense of membership. In several letters, the Beguine Hadewijch has left us testimonies to the intensity of such communities, which included strong emotional attachments between a teacher and her female students, jealousy, rivalries, and also the transmission of psychological insights in the dynamics of spiritual growth.[22] Given comments by Hadewijch and Mechthild, the groups that chose them as leaders and teachers must have operated with some sense of elitism and secrecy. Agnes's anonymous scribe is also concerned about keeping the *vita* itself secret, a desire perhaps not shared by Agnes herself. Mechthild of Magdeburg understood her writings as a teaching tool to be used in her absence; nonetheless, she intended it to

---

[20] See *St. Elisabeth. Fürstin, Dienerin, Heilige*, edited by Phillips Universität Marburg (Sigmaringen: Thorbecke, 1981).

[21] See the introduction to this volume.

[22] See Ulrike Wiethaus, "Female Homoerotic Discourse and Religion in Medieval German Culture", in *Difference and Genders*, edited by Sharon Farmer and Carol Pasternack (Minneapolis: University of Minnesota Press, forthcoming).

be coded in some way. She exhorted her audience to read her books nine times in order to understand them fully. In Christian number symbolism, the numeral nine is most often associated with the nine angelic choirs, but refers also to the mystery of the Trinity.[23] In one of her letters, Hadewijch included a mysterious list of women and men across western Europe whom she considered to be paragons of her own spiritual program of becoming fully human and fully divine, that is to achieve Christlike perfection.[24]

The late Middle Ages witnessed the gradual cultural erosion of the special status granted to holy women, whether behind monastery walls or in public spaces. The decline was caused by a host of factors, both secular and religious. Women specializing in healing became replaced by university-trained male doctors who had little recourse to spiritual tools in their work. As new forms of government and economic exchange changed perceptions of self and community, mysticism gave way to other forms of collectively shared devotion and religious practice. Families relied increasingly on fully institutionalized services of the Church, on local priests and charitable organizations, instead of on a holy woman. With an increase in general literacy and the invention of the printing press, more people had access to pamphlets and tractates and thus were in lesser need of the revelations of religious specialists. But the Church also contributed to these trends through theological efforts to minimize the validity of female mystical experience. Clerics and lay people of both genders gradually associated religious specialists among the laity (both men and women) with witchcraft rather than mysticism.[25] The male professionalization and institutionalization of the cultural and pastoral work of female mystics effectively destroyed their public visibility and performativity.

Despite these changes, the memory of female lay mystics from the Middle Ages has survived, even flourished, in some communities, and inspired and encouraged female religious specialists and their communities in subsequent centuries.[26] The publication of this volume is a testimony to the tenacity of their heritage, even though there is no physical trace of them in what has remained of medieval streets and marketplaces.

---

[23] See Margot Schmidt, *Mechthild of Magdeburg. Das fliessende Licht der Gottheit* (Stuttgart and Bad Cannstatt: Frommann-Holzboog, 1995), 344.

[24] See the introduction to this volume.

[25] See Peter Dinzelbacher, *Heilige oder Hexen? Schicksale auffälliger Frauen im Mittelalter und Frühneuzeit* (Zürich: Artemis & Winkler, 1995).

[26] See Ulrike Wiethaus, "Female Spirituality, Medieval Women, and Commercialism in the United States", in *New Trends in Feminine Spirituality*, 297–315.

Select Bibliography

Primary Sources

de Cantimpré, Thomas. *The Life of Christina Mirabilis*. Translated by Margot King.Toronto: Peregrina Publishing, 1989.

de Vitry, Jacques, and Thomas de Cantimpré. *Two Lives of Marie d'Oignies*. Translated by Margot King and Hugh Feiss. 3rd edition. Toronto: Peregrina Publishing, 1993.

Dinzelbacher, Peter, and Renate, Vogeler. *Leben und Offenbarungen der Wiener Begine Agnes Blannbekin (d. 1315)*. Göppingen: Kümmerle Verlag, 1994.

Ebner, Margarete. *Major Works*. Translated by Leonard Hindsley. New York: Paulist Press, 1993.

Mechthild of Magdeburg. *Das fliessende Licht der Gottheit*. München and Zürich: Artemis Verlag, 1990.

———. *The Flowing Light of the Godhead*. Translated by Frank Tobin. New York: Paulist Press, 1998.

Select Secondary Sources

Atkinson, Clarissa. *The Oldest Vocation: Christian Motherhood in the Middle Ages*. Ithaca: Cornell University Press, 1991.

Barrett, Alexandra. "Undutiful Daughters and Metaphorical Mothers among the Beguines", in *New Trends in Feminine Spirituality: The Holy Women of Liege and their Impact*. Edited by Juliette Dor, Lesley Johnson, and Jocelyn Wogan-Browne. Turnhout, Belg.: Brepols, 1999, 81–105.

Blumenfeld-Kosinski, Renate, and Timea Szell, editors. *Images of Sainthood in Medieval Europe*. Ithaca: Cornell University Press, 1991.

Bynum, Caroline Walker. *The Resurrection of the Body in Western Christianity, 200–1336*. New York: Columbia University Press, 1995.

Chance, Jane. "Speaking *in propria persona*: Authorizing the Subject as a Political Act in Late Medieval Feminine Spirituality", in *New Trends in Feminine Spirituality: The Holy Women of Liege and their Impact*. Edited by Juliette Dor, Lesley Johnson, and Jocelyn Wogan-Browne. Turnhout, Belg.: Brepols, 1999.

Classen, Albrecht. "The Literary Treatment of the Ineffable: Mechthild of Magdeburg, Margaret Ebner, Agnes Blannbekin", *Studies in Spirituality* 8 (1998), 162–87.

Dinzelbacher, Peter. "Die 'Vita et Revelationes' der Wiener Begine Agnes

Blannbekin (d. 1315) im Rahmen der Viten- und Offenbarungsliteratur ihrer Zeit", in *Frauenmystik im Mittelalter.* Edited by Peter Dinzelbacher and Dieter R. Bauer. Ostfildern bei Stuttgart: Schwabenverlag, 1985, 152–78.

————. "Die Wiener Minoriten im ausgehenden 13. Jahrhundert nach dem Urteil der zeitgenössischen Begine Agnes Blannbekin". In *Bettelorden und Stadt. Bettelorden und städtisches Leben im Mittelalter und in der Neuzeit.* Edited by Dieter Berg. Werl: Dietrich Coelde Verlag, 1992, 181–91.

Dor, Juliette, Leslie Johnson, and Jocelyn Wogan-Browne, editors. *New Trends in Feminine Spirituality: The Holy Women of Liège and their Impact.* Turnhout, Belg.: Brepols, 1999.

Ferrante, Joan M. *To the Glory of her Sex: Women's Roles in the Composition of Medieval Texts.* Bloomington and Indianapolis: Indiana University Press, 1997.

Galloway, Penny. "Neither Miraculous nor Astonishing: The Devotional Practices of Beguine Communities in French Flanders". In *New Trends in Feminine Spirituality: The Holy Women of Liege and their Impact.* Edited by Juliette Dor, Lesley Johnson, and Jocelyn Wogan-Browne. Turnhout, Belg.: Brepols, 1999, 107–29.

Grundmann, Herbert. *Religious Movements in the Middle Ages.* Translated by Steven Rowan. Notre Dame: University of Notre Dame Press, 1995. Previously published as *Religöse Bewegungen im Mittelalter.* Leipzig: Ebering Verlag, 1935.

Kadel, Andrew. *Matrology: A Bibliography of Writings by Christian Women from the First to the Fifteenth Centuries.* New York: Continuum, 1995.

McDonnell, Ernest W. *The Beguines and Beghards in Medieval Culture: With Special Emphasis on the Belgian Scene.* New Brunswick: 1954. Reprint New York: Octagon Books, 1969.

McGinn, Bernard. *The Flowering of Mysticism: Men and Women in the New Mysticism (1200–1350).* New York: Crossroad, 1998.

McKelvie, Roberta Agnes. *Retrieving a Living Tradition: Angelina of Montegiove. Franciscan, Tertiary, Beguine.* St. Bonaventure: The Franciscan Institute, 1997.

Mooney, Catherine M. "The Authorial Role of Brother A. in the Composition of Angela of Foligno's Revelations". In *Creative Women in Medieval and Early Modern Italy: A Religious and Artistic Renaissance.* Edited by E. Ann Matter and John Coakley. Philadelphia: University of Pennsylvania Press, 1994, 34–64.

Mulder-Bakker, Anneke B., editor. *Sanctity and Motherhood: Essays on Holy Mothers in the Middle Ages.* New York: Garland, 1995.

Newman, Barbara. *From Virile Woman to WomanChrist: Studies in Medieval Religion and Literature.* Philadelphia: University of Pennsylvania Press, 1995.

Peters, Ursula. *Religiöse Erfahrung als literarisches Faktum. Zur Vorge-*

schichte und Genese frauenmystischer Texte des 13. und 14. Jahrhunderts. Tübingen: Niemeyer Verlag, 1988.

Ringler, Siegfried. *Viten- und Offenbarungsliteratur. Quellen und Studien*. München: Artemis Verlag, 1980.

Rubin, Miri. *Corpus Christi: The Eucharist in Late Medieval Culture*. Cambridge: Cambridge University Press, 1991.

Simons, Walter. "The Beguine Movement in the Southern Low Countries: A Reassessment". *Bulletin de l'Institut historique belge de roi* 59 (1989): 63–105.

Stoklaska, Anneliese. "Die Revelationes der Agnes Blannbekin. Ein mystisches Unikat im Schrifttum des Wiener Mittelalters", *Jahrbuch des Vereins für Geschichte der Stadt Wien* 43 (1987), 7–34.

———. "Weibliche Religiösität im mittelalterlichen Wien unter besonderer Berücksichtigung der Agnes Blannbekin". In *Religiöse Frauenbewegung und mystische Frömmigkeit im Mittelalter*. Edited by Peter Dinzelbacher and Dieter Bauer. Köln and Wien: Böhlau Verlag, 1988, 165–84.

Watt, Diane, editor. *Women in their Communities*. Cardiff: University of Wales Press, 1997.

Index